T0337946

Studies in Economic Reform and Social Justice

LAND:
THE ELUSIVE QUEST FOR SOCIAL JUSTICE, TAXATION REFORM AND A SUSTAINABLE PLANETARY ENVIRONMENT

Philip Day

Blackwell
Publishing

The Series
Studies in Economic Reform and Social Justice

Laurence S. Moss, Series Editor

Robert V. Andelson, ed.
Land-Value Taxation Around the World

Critics of Henry George, 2nd edition, volume 1 (2003)

Critics of Henry George, 2nd edition, volume 2 (2004)

J. A. Giacalone and C. W. Cobb, eds.
*The Path to Justice: Following in the
Footsteps of Henry George*

Christopher K. Ryan
*Harry Gunnison Brown
An Orthodox Economist and His Contributions*

Philip Day
*Land: The Elusive Quest for Social Justice, Taxation Reform
and a Sustainable Planetary Environment*

Studies in Economic Reform and Social Justice

LAND:
THE ELUSIVE QUEST FOR SOCIAL JUSTICE, TAXATION REFORM AND A SUSTAINABLE PLANETARY ENVIRONMENT

By
Philip Day

Series Editor
Laurence S. Moss

Blackwell
Publishing

350 Main Street, Malden, MA 02148-5020, USA
9600 Garsington Road, Oxford OX4 2DQ, UK
550 Swanston Street, Carlton, Victoria 3053, Australia

First published 2005 by Blackwell Publishing Ltd.

Library of Congress Cataloging-in-Publication Data
Day, Philip, 1924–
    Land : the elusive quest for social justice, taxation reform &
a sustainable planetary environment / Philip Day.
        p. cm.—(Studies in economic reform and social justice)
    Includes bibliographical references and index.
    ISBN-13: 978-1-4051-4977-8 (casebound)
    ISBN-10: 1-4051-4977-9 (casebound)
    ISBN-13: 978-1-4051-4978-5 (pbk.)
    ISBN-10: 1-4051-4978-7 (pbk.)
    1. Land use—Social aspects—Australia. 2. Land use—
Economicl aspects—Australia. 3. Land use—Environmental
aspects—Australia. 4. Sustainable development—Australia.
I. Title. II. Series.
HD1036.D39 2005
333.730994—dc22
                                                    2005055311

A catalogue record for this title is available from the Library of
Congress.

Set in 10 on 13pt Garamond Light
by SNP Best-set Typesetter Ltd., Hong Kong
Printed and bound in the United States
by the Sheridan Press

For further information on
Blackwell Publishing, visit our website:
http://www.blackwellpublishing.com

"I conceive that land belongs to a vast family of whom many are dead, some are living, & countless millions are still unborn."

—An unknown Nigerian Chief

Dr. Philip Day. See p. 111 for an autobiographical sketch.

Contents

Frontispiece. vi

Foreword ix

Preface xi

1. The Subversion of Reason 1

2. Institutionalised Profiteering 9

3. The Diversion of Investment 25

4. The Employment Mirage 29

5. Fiscal Masochism 35

6. Resourcing Public Revenue 39

7. Underpinning a Global Morality 55

8. The Essential Requirements 61

9. Impediments and Counter-Arguments 65

10. Henry George Re-Visited 73

11. Apathy, Cupidity or Conspiracy? 85

12. The Enduring Enigma 95

Postscript 99

References 109

Autobiographical Sketch of Philip Denny
Day (1924–) 111

Index 115

Foreword

It gives me great pleasure to introduce this erudite and eminently readable book as another in our series "Studies in Economic Reform and Social Justice." Captain James Cook claimed Australia for England in 1770 and from that point on an individual-rights-oriented privatized system of land ownership replaced the communal understanding of land that had long prevailed among the Aboriginal Australians. There would be no lasting harm here if only the privatized owners paid a tax based on the unimproved value of that land but they do not pay such a tax. Community land management and approved changes in land use spring into capital gains that are captured by a lucky few. And in some cases by a corrupt few. The community as a whole loses as a few well-connected or astute speculators reap gains where they have not sown.

There is a moral norm implicit in the discussions that make up this valued series of books. That moral norm is simply stated in the following way—"no one should be permitted to make an unearned profit merely from acquiring possession of land [because land is] a natural resource that no man has created" [see Day's discussion on p. 14, below]. And if that moral argument does not convince the reader, then perhaps a pure economic efficiency argument might serve just as well. That efficiency argument is simply that since land is given more or less in fixed supply, the imposition of a tax on the unimproved value of land will have no adverse effects on the allocation of resources (neither land nor any other resources will have to be shifted around, especially if we ignore wealth changes resulting from the first initiation of that tax). If the yields from the land value tax are ample enough, then most other taxes on income, inheritance, corporate profits, and, especially, the excise tax on consumer goods can be eliminated or at least substantially reduced. This will result in a net increase in social well-being and only require that landowners use their land in the most valued ways.

This version of the Day book augments a previous Australian edition of *Land* by including some timely information about the reconciliation efforts now underway in Australia to recognize the rights of the Aboriginals to selected ancestral lands Aboriginal culture understands land as something owned by the entire community. The "fee simple" idea from medieval Europe when it is used in support of Aboriginal interests can at best only narrow the gap but never reconcile completely the radically different manners in which land is viewed by the two communities.

We are grateful to Day for allowing us to include his marvelously well-argued book in our ongoing series.

Laurence S. Moss
Babson College, 2005

Preface

INFLUENCED BY THE proliferation of paper competing for public attention and, perhaps presumptuously, by a sense of urgency, *Land* has been kept within modest bounds. It has been distilled from a wealth of available material from which the argument could have been further reinforced, but at the risk of diminished readability. While the particular circumstances prevailing in Australia have served as a convenient case study, it is hoped that the central issues have a wider relevance and applicability. Chapter 1 is an expanded version of a talk broadcast in February 1994 in the *Ockham's Razor* series of Radio National's Science Program. Other chapters draw on earlier work. In particular, on *Land Value Capture*, a report prepared in 1992 for the Local Government Association of Queensland; on a report on *Town Planning and the Land Market* prepared in 1993 for Gostroi, the Russian government's ministry of town planning and construction; and on the 1989 report of the Lord Mayor of Brisbane's Committee of Inquiry into Valuation and Rating, of which I was privileged to be a member and research coordinator.

In addition, however, I am indebted to numerous professional colleagues, especially those who collaborated in the preparation of *Town Planning and the Land Market*. And I am indebted to the Henry George Foundation (Australia), which met the cost of my participation in a multi-national delegation to the former Soviet Union in October–November 1993. Responsibility for shortcomings of commission and omission is, of course, mine alone.

Philip Day
Brisbane, March 1995

A postscript reviews the history of Australian land law, recent tax "reform" and in particular the emergent issue of Aboriginal land "rights" following recent landmark decisions of the Australian High Court.

(In 1997, *Land* was translated and disseminated by Ecograd, a Russian urban research organisation in St Petersburg.)

Philip Day
January 2003

Words importing the male gender (for the sake of brevity) are intended equally to import the female gender.

The AMERICAN JOURNAL of ECONOMICS and SOCIOLOGY

Published QUARTERLY in the interest of constructive synthesis in the social sciences, under grants from the FRANCIS NEILSON Fund and the ROBERT SCHALKENBACH FOUNDATION. Founded in 1941

| Volume 64 | November, 2005 | Number 5 |

Chapter 1

The Subversion of Reason

THIS BOOK IS ABOUT AN ENIGMA.

It is concerned with the mystery of how vast wealth is made and disbursed within a tangled maze of institutional arrangements and practices—practices that are seemingly pre-ordained, notwithstanding their manifestly questionable consequences for the welfare of society. The enigma that the book addresses is the mindset that sustains and acquiesces in this phenomenon, a phenomenon that has prevailed for centuries, challenged but not seriously threatened.

The following pages seek to discover whether the mindset does indeed reflect an inescapable order of things that can never be otherwise. A pretentious undertaking, perhaps. Yet the time seems opportune to review the evidence across interdisciplinary professional boundaries from a late 20th-century viewpoint.

More specifically, the focus is on land. In the first instance, the chapters that follow focus on the bestowing of windfall profits on

American Journal of Economics and Sociology, Vol. 64, No. 5 (November, 2005).
© 2005 American Journal of Economics and Sociology, Inc.

landowners by a curiously ambivalent society—a society whose conscience is disturbed on the one hand by the intractability of mounting structural unemployment and the assumed need to promote more
development and, on the other hand, by the impact of growth
and development upon a fragile planetary environment. The social,
economic and environmental consequences are reviewed. It will
be shown that profits from land contribute, among other things, to
increasing inequality and the polarisation of the rich and the poor,
the erosion of environmental resources, the underfunding of public
infrastructure and services and, not least, to inordinate reliance upon
a taxation system that penalises the virtues of hard work and enterprise which society purports to value and encourage.

Thus the argument centres upon society's attitude to land and the
profits that can be made from acquiring and dealing in land. The
enigma is the survival of this societal attitude in spite of the damag-
ing consequences that demonstrably flow from it.

For those who are prepared to persevere, exploring the enigma
involves seeking clues along a complicated and labyrinthine trail. In
the first instance, however, the issues can be confronted by drawing
upon familiar phenomena using contemporary Australian society as
a case study.

A familiar enough starting point is the benefit historically conferred
on "lucky" landholders when public works are undertaken in their
vicinity, when roads or railways are extended and land is "opened
up" for more intensive development. Public funds are expended.
Private land values are increased. And the element of luck can be
eliminated by prior knowledge and political manipulation. A small
part of the windfall benefit is subsequently siphoned off when public
authorities revalue the land and the landholder pays local government rates (and possibly state land tax) on his or her increased valuation. But these annual levies are only a few cents in the dollar. The
bulk of the increased land value accrues to the landholder as an
unearned gift from the community. And the value of his holding con-
tinues to increase thereafter as the population grows and the community develops.

A more dramatic phenomenon is the *overnight* increase in land
value that occurs when planning approval is obtained to use land for

a more intensive use. For example, when approval is given to sub-divide farmland for housing, or to convert a house site to shops or a block of flats. Or to convert coastal bushland to a "resort." The approval, or permit, is valuable. It is valuable irrespective of whether the actual development of the land is subsequently profitable—or even if it is not carried out at all. The land can be sold, with the approval, for a great deal more than it was previously worth. Yet the landholder has done nothing except apply for approval to change the use. It is the public planning authority's decision that has changed the land value—literally by the stroke of a pen, or by changing the colour on a zoning map.

But the matter does not end there. Its consequences are disturb-ing, and their tentacles extend throughout society. For one thing, in the case of a town planning approval the increase in land value is quite literally inflationary. Because of the approval the land increases in money value, but there has been no commensurate increase in goods or services. Thus the windfall increase in land value is a built-in contribution to inflation that is passed on to all subsequent purchasers. For homeseekers or intending commercial or industrial entrepreneurs, land becomes less affordable.

Another consequence has disturbing implications for the environ-ment. The prospect of a windfall increase in land value operates as a standing invitation to "develop" land by seeking approval for a change of use—regardless of whether the proposed development is genuinely needed. Which means that, irrespective of its environmen-tal significance, or the need to maintain some clear demarcation between town and country and curb the environmentally destructive process of urban sprawl, *all* land becomes vulnerable to entrepre-neurial initiatives.

A town planning scheme may purport to preserve certain land uses. It may designate certain land "non-urban," for example. But planning agencies are not immune from developers' persuasion. Or from political pressures—sometimes plausibly supporting employment-generating development, sometimes less charitably motivated. And in borderline circumstances the integrity of town planning schemes is inherently difficult to maintain. For example, where a landowner on one side of an arbitrary zoning boundary line is denied the opportunity to sell out at a substantial profit that the plan confers upon his neighbour on the other side of the boundary line.

Town planning *theory* is impeccable. It has always maintained that land value increases resulting from public planning decisions should be recouped on behalf of the community whose public agencies have created them. Town planning theory requires that this so-called betterment should be recouped from landowners. And, conversely, town planning theory asserts that any detriment or "worsenment" that town planning decisions impose on landowners should be compensated. On both counts, however, practice falls notoriously short of theory.[1]

In 1976, Australia, along with other nations, endorsed the so-called Vancouver Plan, the recommendations of the United Nations Habitat Conference on Human Settlements, which called for the unearned increment in land values resulting from changes in land use to be recouped by communities and applied to the provision of urban infrastructure and services. Nowhere in the Western world, however, has this obligation to recoup betterment been fully implemented.

The reality of this situation is obscured by the fact that in practice (but not always) some contribution to infrastructure and services is required from development applicants as a condition of their being granted planning approval. But the amount of contribution is not related to the increase in land value. So-called developer contributions are "negotiated" by local government councils, arbitrarily and haphazardly, and seldom in pursuance of any clear-cut philosophy or rationale. Because interdisciplinary boundaries have tended to compartmentalise town planning, land valuation and public revenue raising, an esoteric area of public administration has escaped the strictures of latter-day economic rationalism and is characterised in practice by quite extraordinary anomalies and incongruities.

What it amounts to is that, by providing a regular mechanism for approving changes in land use, town planning systems actually legitimise the conferring of windfall profits upon "lucky" private landowners or upon developers acting on their behalf. Which means that, to the extent that these windfall increases in land value are not offset by contributions to community works and services, all development applicants receive a windfall bonus. There is thus an element of hidden subsidy or government-granted privilege in virtually every development approval—*the development industry is quite literally subsidised by the community.*

The irony of this should not pass unnoticed. Developers see themselves in the entrepreneurial vanguard of the free enterprise system. Yet speculative profiteering in land violates one of the cardinal principles of free enterprise: it rewards non-producers rather than producers.

In the circumstances, precise quantification of these windfall profits is impossible. To put the matter in some perspective, however, in Australia there are currently over 750 local government councils charged with controlling development in their respective communities. While not a great deal of developmental activity takes place in the smaller rural shires, the councils in urban areas (together with state governments, which frequently assume responsibility for "major" projects) collectively handle huge numbers of development applications every year, generating multi-million dollar increases in land value for landowning individuals and corporations. In a submission to the Industry Commission in 1992, the National Capital Planning Authority estimated that the betterment being forgone throughout Australia—wealth that could fund the backlog of urban infrastructure and community services—was in the order of at least $3–400 million annually.[2]

It comes as no surprise, therefore, that Australian savings are being diverted disproportionately into land and property at the expense of investment in more productive activities, as an Economic Planning Advisory Council research paper confirmed in 1993.[3] The tax system is demonstrably biased against genuinely productive investment. Nor is it surprising (as the statistics in Chapter 3 confirm) that speculative investment in land played a major part in fuelling the boom of the late 1980s, which wrought such social and economic havoc when it collapsed.

As for the other side of the coin, the perception—often acknowledged (but timorously shied away from) by government spokespeople—that betterment is not being recouped—tends to influence governmental attitudes to compensation. Thus there is a disposition to resist paying compensation to landowners whose land is devalued by planning decisions (such as a decision to "down zone" their land from, say, "high density residential" to "low density residential"). And currently in Australia there is no entitlement at all to compensation for landowners whose properties are devalued by the proximity of new public works (such as freeways).[4] Yet, in reality, if they were recouped, the "windfalls"—to use the American terminology—could pay for the occasional "wipeouts" many times over.

In passing, there is perverse irony in the fact that, in cases where landowners are successful in claiming compensation for the acquisition of their properties, or for down-zoning, the amount of compensation paid from the public purse is assessed on market values, *which, in the case of the land component, have previously been created by public planning decisions or community development.*

Clearly, the issues hinge around the ownership and use of land and, by implication, the derivation of public revenue. The underlying assumption is that land, which is provided by nature and is in finite supply, may nevertheless be owned and dealt with on the same basis as any man-made commodity. Yet, while this assumption goes to the heart of the matter, there is nothing pre-ordained or inviolate about it. Tribal societies, including Aboriginal society in Australia, have never subscribed to it. In the case of Anglo-Australian society, it originated in the Middle Ages when baronial landholders asserted the right to hold land outright instead of conditionally upon their providing services to the feudal kings. Thereafter, in lieu of contributed services, the needs of government had to be met instead by taxation.

Subsequent chapters canvass the implications of this in more detail. Some traces of the notion of land being ultimately vested in the Crown on behalf of the community still linger. Thus in the early years of European settlement in Australia grants of land were made subject to the payment of a (small) "quit-rent," which notionally recognised the landholder's obligation to the Crown. And land that has not been acquired outright by individual citizens is recognised as Crown land. To a minor degree the notion of landholders' indebtedness to the community is also reflected in Australia (and other Western societies) in local government rates levied on property and in state land taxes. Nevertheless, by far the largest proportion of public revenue, indeed, currently an increasing proportion, is raised by other means—in

Australia, for example, by income and sales taxes levied pursuant to the 6,700-odd pages of the Income Tax Assessment Act and associated legislation.

That land is taxed lightly is no mystery. Until the franchise was extended by stages during the 19th century, the governing classes in all Western societies were typically major landowners. Indeed, there are no mysteries about any of the matters traversed in the foregoing pages. They may not have been drawn together in one document, but the facts are well enough known to all those conversant with land planning and development practice.

The real mystery is that of the societal mindset that seemingly accepts as inevitable and unalterable a situation that, to summarise:

- permits land value increases created by public agencies to be privately appropriated;
- tolerates the inflationary impact of land value increases that render access to land less affordable;
- perpetuates inequality by enabling landed wealth, once acquired, to increase exponentially with population growth and community development;
- encourages speculative investment in land and property—rather than investment in the production of goods and services;
- accepts the co-existence of private wealth and under-funded community services and facilities;
- exacerbates the difficulties of reconciliation with indigenous peoples;
- mocks the pursuit of ecological sustainability by putting a premium on the infinite continuance of land "development"; and
- penalises productive activities by taxing the rewards of labour and enterprise rather than taxing the private consumption of a community resource.

If features such as these are indeed endemic, the picture they present of a Western-style market economy is not a pretty one. Notwithstanding the institutional and regulatory safeguards with which an established democratic culture has tempered free market capitalism in Western societies over the past century or more, its dominant characteristics remain greed and self-interest. Inevitably it prompts the question whether it is the best alternative the Western world can offer the peoples of eastern Europe and the former Soviet Union who are endeavouring—without the same cultural and institutional background—to discard the shackles of an even more discreditable economic system (the demise of which may owe as much to the triumph of incipient democracy over dictatorship as to any confidently perceived superiority of capitalism over socialism).

Such speculation is profoundly disturbing. But the ultimate enigma is the fact that the flawed logic underlying Western land management and economic practice was exposed more than a century ago by a political economist and social philosopher whose writing attracted universal attention. His central argument has never been convincingly refuted. Yet the solution he propounded has never been accepted and implemented.

Readers may pass quickly over the next chapter if they do not require a more detailed account of the shortcomings of the land use planning system. Subsequent chapters canvass the prospects and prerequisites of remedial action in a late 20th-century context. The concluding chapters seek clues to the enigma among a maze of misconceptions and misinterpretations, and occasional intimations of conspiracy. They note some adventitious circumstances that have influenced the course of economic history; and they speculate about whether the enigma of a patently flawed but obdurately persistent mindset may defy any attempt to unravel and unmask it.

Supplementary Notes

1. American planning literature prefers the more colourful terms "windfalls" and "wipeouts."

2. Industry Commission, *Taxation and Financial Policy Impacts on Urban Settlement*, Volume 1, AGPS, Canberra, 1993, p. 385.

3. Research Paper No. 34, *Income Tax and Asset Choice in Australia*, AGPS, Canberra, 1993.

4. If their properties are not actually acquired, property owners receive no compensation for "injurious affection" (for example, by noise, pollution or loss of visual amenity in the case of an adjacent freeway). An incidental consequence of this is that, in comparative assessments of public transport and freeway costs, the latter tend to be understated because no allowance need be included for compensation.

Chapter 2

Institutionalised Profiteering

THE RELATIONSHIP BETWEEN urban and regional planning (conveniently but misleadingly abbreviated to "town planning" and in recent years more compendiously described as "environmental planning") and the land market is critically important economically, socially and environmentally. For many reasons, however, the relationship, together with its implications for equitable and efficient public revenue raising, is not always clearly understood.

Throughout history the conscious location of dwellings, roads and community buildings has been, in effect, a form of town planning. In their different ways architects, builders, engineers and surveyors have all contributed. But it is only in comparatively recent times that town planning has become recognised as a separate profession, a profession that tries to co-ordinate the activities of all the other more specialised professions involved in building and maintaining human settlements. It is, of course, essentially a *public* activity concerned with the public interest. Its objectives are to promote safe, healthy, convenient, aesthetically satisfying and economically efficient and environmentally responsible human settlements. These are public functions. The extent to which these public objectives are achieved will depend upon the political will of public authorities and upon the extent of the professional town planning resources available to them.

Town planning may be pro-active, in the sense of positively guiding the direction of future development. Or it may merely react to privately initiated development proposals. Potentially, however, town planning has an enormous influence because it operates by *controlling the use of land* upon which all human activities are ultimately based.

In the broadest sense, controlling the use of land is a national responsibility. It is therefore a proper function of national govern-

American Journal of Economics and Sociology, Vol. 64, No. 5 (November, 2005).
© 2005 American Journal of Economics and Sociology, Inc.

ments to formulate strategic land use plans and policies. For example, in respect of balanced population distribution, the curbing of excessive city growth, promoting regional industrial development, efficient transport provision and the conservation of environmental resources. At the other end of the spectrum, and subject to overall national planning policies, land use planning at a detailed level is the proper responsibility of local government. At a national or regional level, plans may take the form of policy statements, perhaps accompanied by broad diagrammatic maps. At a local level, plans will take the form of detailed local policy statements accompanied by detailed minimum standards for particular kinds of land use, together with detailed maps (showing property boundaries) indicating where particular land uses should be located (or not located). A common technique is to designate zones for estimated land use needs, for example, for agriculture, housing, industry, commerce, public facilities and recreation. If sufficient professional resources are available, a better technique is to describe in written detail the intended future character of the various parts of a local government area. The rigour of town planning laws will depend upon the philosophy of the government of the day.

There is no definitive form of town plan. A town plan can take various forms depending on the size of the area and the planning resources available. In essence, however, a town plan is a statement of planning principles and an expression of a community's desired objectives, adopted after consultation with the people of the area and taking account of their aspirations. It will be accompanied by a statement of the ways and means by which the objectives of the plan will be achieved. For example, by the designation of what land uses are permissible, and by adopting minimum allotment sizes, maximum building heights, noise and pollution standards, landscaping standards and motor vehicle parking standards. *Regulating the use to which land can be put will obviously have a major bearing upon its value.*

Town planning in Western societies has achieved—or partly achieved—some very desirable objectives. For example:

- It has segregated incompatible land uses, such as housing and noxious industries.

- It has restrained urban encroachment upon valuable agricultural land and upon land containing useful extractive minerals such as sand, gravel and coal.
- It has prevented urban development on unsuitable land such as land subject to flooding or subsidence, and thereby minimised the risk of public authorities being called upon to undertake costly rescue and rehabilitation operations.
- It has prevented "ribbon-type" commercial development from reducing the capacity of major roads to carry the volume of through traffic for which they were designed and built (at considerable public cost).
- It has promoted the development of alternative commercial sub-centres to relieve the pressures upon the central business districts of major cities and make employment opportunities more accessible to people in the suburbs.
- Particularly in the United Kingdom, it has led to the successful creation of self-contained new towns to relieve the concentration of population in large cities such as London, Birmingham and Glasgow.
- In the United Kingdom it has also successfully preserved a clear distinction between urban development and the natural countryside.
- It has helped to co-ordinate the provision of public works and services (such as schools, hospitals and transport) in anticipation of future demand.
- It has required private developers to make some contribution to public works and services needed as a consequence of their development proposals.
- It has promoted better quality urban development by requiring higher standards of design and landscaping and by the provision of parks and open spaces and improved facilities for cyclists and pedestrians.

The list is not exhaustive. Yet in some important respects, town planning in Western societies is fatally flawed. When, in the course of administering town planning, a public planning authority approves an application by or on behalf of a landholder to use land for a more intensive use, *the value of the land is increased.* Thus, if approval is given to convert rural land to residential or commercial use, the market value of the land will be very considerably increased. But, although the increase in land value is attributable to the public authority's decision, *the increase in land value becomes a gratuitous gift to the private landholder.* The inflationary and environmental implications of this have been alluded to in the previous chapter. Alternatively, the expectation of making a *future* profit can induce landholders to withhold their land from use, thus forcing legitimate urban expansion to "leap-frog" further outward into the hinterland and increasing the cost of extending urban services and infrastructure.

The scope for profiting from land makes it difficult to maintain the integrity of a town plan because of the pressures brought to bear on planning authorities by landowners and developers to have their land "released." And obviously the integrity of town planning can be undermined if people have access to "inside" knowledge about proposed changes to a town plan. For example, a proposal to designate more land to provide for urban expansion. Someone with prior knowledge of the planning authority's intentions can buy the land before the changes are made and subsequently make a substantial profit. Proposed changes to a town plan therefore need to be kept secret. Yet town planning is a public activity that ought to be conducted in open consultation with the community. If not, the principle of public participation in planning is subverted.

In practice, sadly, town plans have commonly been referred to as "speculators' guides."

If the prospective profits from a change in land use are large enough, the integrity of the planning system may be subverted in a different sense. The nature or the location of the development proposed may not conform with the planning agency's plans for the area, but the applicant may be able to afford to offer a persuasive inducement to the planning agency to depart from planning principles. In one recorded case the proponents of a major shopping centre made an offer that the Brisbane City Council is reported to have considered "too good to refuse"—notwithstanding the unsatisfactory traffic situation that was likely to be generated.[1] In the United Kingdom the practice of councils negotiating offers of "planning gain" from proponents of development has reached a stage that some observers equate with simply selling planning permission.

This of course is not to say that the permissible uses of land should never be varied. Town planning must be a dynamic process capable of responding to social and economic change. Development warranted by population growth will require the conversion of more land to urban use and/or the conversion of existing urban land to more intensive urban use. But, if the land use conversion process holds out the prospect of a profit, not from actual development, but from the mere approval of a change of use, it invites applications for a change of use *regardless of whether the proposed development is justified by public needs or market demand.* And once a land use change has been approved, the land can then be sold at an inflated price.

Clearly, town planning systems must provide for and regularise changes in land use. As it currently operates, however, town planning carries within it the seeds of its own emasculation. Well-intentioned planning controls can succumb to a "domino effect" in a variety of urban and rural situations that are inherently inconsis-tent with environmental responsibility and the concept of sustainable development. And, what needs to be stressed, is that *profiting from land is cumulative.* As the history of speculative land dealings amply demonstrates, private fortunes can be made—fortuitously or other-wise—and, once made, land profits accumulate thereafter as the value of land increases as a result of further population growth and incremental community development. In spite of their increasing sophistication, town planning schemes are currently legitimising this phenomenon. *Officially approved land use changes are legitimising private profit-making at the expense of the community.*

The impact of increasing land values on the affordability of domestic housing is a perennial cause for public concern. Because the house building industry is responsive to supply and demand and is highly competitive, it is the increasing price of *land* rather than the cost of building houses that is causing housing to become less affordable for ordinary citizens. This in turn forces lower income citizens—who are least able to afford private transport—to seek cheaper land further away from urban centres (and further away from public transport and other community services and facilities). Thus it aggravates "urban sprawl," and urban services, especially transport, eventually have to be provided over uneconomic distances.

The incongruities of the prevailing situation have not gone unrecognised. Logic and morality are insistent reminders that no one should be permitted to make an unearned profit merely from acquiring possession of land, a natural resource that no man has created. Nevertheless, there has been a reluctance to acknowledge the unique character of land. The picture of responses to the problems that have been described is a curious montage of partial remedies, anomalies and inconsistencies.

One of the tantalising features of the situation is that there is nothing new about it. While town planning in practice has been defective, town planning theory has been logically consistent. It has always recognised the need to recoup benefit and compensate detriment. Thus early English town planning legislation provided that local authorities could claim a percentage of the amount by which the value of a property was increased through the operation of a town planning scheme. Modelled on English precedents, early Australian town planning legislation contained similar provisions enabling local authorities to claim "betterment."[2] But the power to claim betterment was never exercised then, and betterment levies have never operated since, except briefly in New South Wales between 1970 and 1973, and currently in the Australian Capital Territory. (In 1969, NSW enacted legislation to capture 30 percent of the increase in value when rural land around Sydney was rezoned for urban use. The betterment levy raised some $A9 million for public works and services needed for the rezoned land, but the legislation was repealed in 1973 following lobbying by vested interests.)

In the United Kingdom, radically new planning legislation in 1947 attempted to capture 100 percent of the betterment and thereby raise public revenue to provide the public infrastructure needed for postwar reconstruction. However, the betterment provisions of the 1947 Act were repealed in 1953. Subsequent Labour governments attempted to achieve similar objectives, but in every case these attempts were reversed by Conservative governments.

In 1967, the NSW Royal Commission of Inquiry into Rating, Valuation and Local Government Finance recommended the recoupment of betterment. The Commonwealth Commission of Inquiry into Land Tenures (a leading member of which incidentally was the chairman of Australia's largest private development corporation) did likewise in 1974; and so did the NSW Planning and Environment Commission in 1975. So did the UN Habitat Conference in 1976.

In the event, however, betterment levies have been resisted, seemingly for a mixture of reasons (one being that the "before" value may have already anticipated a change of use). Yet some of these reasons no longer apply. For example, the uncertain status of early town planning controls and their limited geographical application; the unfamiliarity of some planning jurisdictions (notably in the United Kingdom) with the concept of valuing *unimproved* land; and the limited capacity generally of public valuing authorities until fairly recent times to maintain frequent and up-to-date valuations of all land.

In practice the twin problems of betterment and compensation have never been comprehensively confronted. *Until they are resolved, town planning will remain fundamentally flawed.*[3]

In the absence of betterment levies, what has happened over the years in Australia, the United Kingdom, the United States and other Western countries is that the perennial shortage of public sector funds for providing urban infrastructure has led to the adoption of other methods of capturing, in effect, at least *some* of the increase in land values accruing from approved changes in land use. When dealing with development applications involving a change to a more intense and valuable land use, public planning authorities have *negotiated* with development applicants (that is, with landholders or developers acting on their behalf or holding options to purchase). They have negotiated contributions to community infrastructure as a condition of granting planning approval. In Australia, this process of negotiating "development contributions" has had a long and complicated history. It started with requiring the subdividers of private land to donate a percentage of the land for public parks and recreation. Over time the process has been extended and applicants for development approval may be required to undertake the provision of roads, drainage, water and sewerage services and various community facilities, or pay a money contribution in lieu. The process has evolved and is still evolving. Not surprisingly, in the United Kingdom, where negotiating "planning gain" or "community benefit" is akin to selling planning approval, local planning agencies require considerable negotiating skills and sophisticated financial expertise.

In Australia, the six state governments have experimented with various ways of regulating the extent to which local governments, in their role of local planning authorities, can require these development contributions. Depending on their attitude to private enterprise and the political influence of the development industry, state governments have placed limits on the kinds of development contributions that local planning authorities can require, and upon the circumstances in which they can be required. At the same time they too have been conscious of the pressing need to secure the provision of adequate urban infrastructure for an expanding population; and in the case of major developmental projects for which they have assumed direct responsibility, state governments have similarly negotiated with the proponents of development.

Over the course of the post-war years there has thus been a general, if curiously ambivalent, acceptance of the notion of requiring the proponents of development projects to contribute to some degree by way of providing works and services and/or cash in lieu. But the reasons for extracting development contributions have never been clearly stated. The motivation has variously stemmed from the incapacity of local government councils to provide the urban infrastructure needed by a rapidly expanding urban population (particularly in the early post-war years); from a general disposition to transfer responsibility for infrastructure from the public sector to the private sector as far as possible; and from a recognition—not precisely articulated—that somehow developers can afford to contribute. These motivations have been reinforced by the fact—again not precisely articulated (but very evident in the United Kingdom)—that a public planning authority may have very considerable bargaining power vis-à-vis a development applicant seeking favourable (and expeditious) consideration of his development application.

In the event the negotiation of development contributions has been arbitrary, uneven and haphazard. Negotiation behind closed doors prior to the formalising of approval is obviously open to corruption. It is based on no clearly defined rationale: the amount of contribution required from development applicants is *not directly related to the amount of the increase in land value that will accrue to them as a result of obtaining planning approval.* In other words, development contributions offset only part of the windfall profit. Only in the case of the ACT betterment levy is there an implicit acknowledgement that, where public action confers a monetary benefit in the form of increased land value, at least some part of this betterment should be recouped from the beneficiaries and rightly appropriated by the community.[4] Nowhere else in Australia is the rationale for requiring some contribution from development applicants spelt out. The situation is characterised by ambivalence and indecision.[5]

Present Queensland legislation contains fairly specific provisions enabling local authorities to require contributions from development applicants in respect of water and sewerage headworks. In other respects, however, it requires that any contributions to works and services "external" to the applicant's actual development must be "reasonable" and be "relevant" to the proposed development. There must be a "nexus." Until recently, Victorian legislation provided for contributions only in fairly limited circumstances. NSW legislation, currently the most explicit, goes further and specifically authorises local authorities to require contributions to certain kinds of community facilities. Nevertheless, a nexus must be demonstrated.

There are inherent difficulties common to the development contributions approach as currently practised. They stem from both the lack of any clearly expressed rationale and the lack of any definitive criteria for determining the precise *amount* of contribution. Thus one major difficulty is that the practice involves value judgements about what is "reasonable" and what is "relevant." These questions are therefore exposed to debate in the courts or appeals tribunals. Particularly in Queensland, the high cost of legal proceedings in the Planning and Environment Court operates to deter local authorities from requiring contributions as extensive as those they might otherwise consider it appropriate to require.

Secondly, because there are no quantitative criteria for determining the amount of contribution, the development applicant and the planning authority are placed in a bargaining position with an inherent potential for corruption. A problem for smaller local authorities is their limited professional capacity to determine (or guess) what contribution a sophisticated development proposal can reasonably be expected to sustain. In the United Kingdom this has led to the emergence of consultants who specialise in assisting councils to assess the economic viability of development proposals so that they can gauge the amount of "planning gain" that they may be able to negotiate. This in turn highlights another unsatisfactory feature of the development contributions process as currently practised: if development contributions are assessed, not on the increased land value, but on the estimated profitability of the actual development proposed, they then become a de facto extra tax on enterprise—an outcome incompatible with the economic policy objectives that most communities profess to espouse.

These difficulties and the absence of any clearly understood rationale explain why the practice of extracting development contributions varies widely among local authorities. As recent studies in Queensland and NSW have disclosed, a surprising number of councils do not extract any contributions at all. Nevertheless, while the practice of requiring development contributions is patently haphazard and ill-defined, the fact that present Australian planning systems enable, even if they do not systematically require, *some* portion of the land value increase to be recouped or offset has unfortunately obscured the central issue. *The compelling logic of capturing the windfall profits conferred by publicly authorised changes in land use—and capturing them in full—has been lost sight of along the way.*

The issue is further clouded by the plausible special pleading that the development industry has successfully propagated. While they protest occasionally (but not very loudly), developers are prepared to accept development contributions as a "necessary evil." Nevertheless, they assert that they need some land value profit as an "incentive" to develop. In other words, unlike other producers of goods and services who must rely on the competitive quality of their products and the market demand for them, the development industry is unwilling to rely on the market demand for its developments. It asserts a need to profit, *additionally*, from a natural community resource, namely, raw land. Thus, to the extent that development contributions do not recoup the whole of the land value increase, *the development industry is effectively subsidised by the community*—whether or not its products are actually needed. It claims entitlement to an unspecific open-ended incentive derived from exploiting a natural resource.

Another plausible notion that the development industry is disposed to foster is that imposing development contributions or other charges increases the cost of land and housing to the "battling" end consumer. This is a mischievous myth because the liability for rates or levies upon land *reduces* the price that the vendor of raw (undeveloped) land can ask an intending developer to pay (unless the vendor enjoys an absolute monopoly of supply and can demand to be indemnified against a development levy). The affordability thereafter of *developed* land and housing will depend upon the *standard* of the infrastructural development provided to meet prevailing community expectations or government requirements (irrespective of the mode of funding it).

The situation is further confused because there is a separate, additional reason for requiring developers to make some contribution to the provision of public infrastructure. Every development proposed is likely to have some impact on the community. In order to minimise adverse environmental impacts, town planning conditions are therefore imposed in respect of such things as allotment size, building height and the provision of landscaping. But a new development proposal is also likely to have an economic impact upon the existing community. Thus a proposal to erect a multi-storey office building or a multi-storey residential building may mean that public authorities must, as a consequence, enlarge existing water and sewerage services, or provide more road space or vehicle parking space. In other words, there are consequential costs that the community will have to meet. This has led—mainly in parts of the United States—to the practice of requiring developers to pay "impact fees" to offset these consequential costs.

While the concept of impact fees has not yet been fully embraced in Australia, the logic of assessing the economic impact of development proposals on the community and identifying the liability of their proponents for whatever consequential augmentation of existing community facilities and services is attributable to their proposals is indisputable. All development proposals should logically be automatically subject to impact fees. (If a particular development proposal is desirable in the public interest but is not economically viable, the impact fees can be wholly or partially waived.) But, impact fees are not related to land values. Recouping the consequences of such impacts is not the same as recouping land value increases attributable to planning approval. Thus, development contributions (or betterment levies) and impact fees should be clearly distinguished. In practice, however, they are not, and responsibilities and obligations are blurred.

It may be appropriate at this point to emphasise that uncaptured betterment tends to contribute to urban sprawl in three ways. The inflationary impact on land value of development approval renders land generally less affordable and induces lower income homeseekers to move further out and accept (for the time being) minimal urban services and facilities. Secondly, the prospect of increased windfall profits induces some landholders to withhold vacant land from the market and force new development to "leapfrog" their land and move further out. Thirdly, the cost of outer urban development tends for several reasons to be understated. Whatever urban infrastructure is contributed by developers will be limited to works and services that are within the responsibility of local government and within its powers (or inclination) to require. End consumers of homesites are likely to escape having to meet the *full* cost of infrastructure provided by *local* government, and they will escape contributing to the cost of infrastructure provided in due course by *other levels of government.* By contrast, in addition to a locational premium, the value of *all* urban infrastructure will have long since been capitalised in the price of developed land in inner urban areas.

While development application approvals and planning scheme rezonings are the source of the most dramatic windfall increases in land value, there are other ways in which fortuitous private profits are conferred upon landowners. Thus, when a public authority constructs public works (such as a railway or a major road or an irrigation dam), the value of land in the vicinity is likely to be increased. As Judge Foster observed in the Arbitration Court in 1947, Australia's railways would be in credit, and not saddled with enormous capital debts, if they had been credited with the increase in land values that they (and not the landowners) had created.[6]

A further cause of land value increases is, of course, simply incremental community development in response to population growth.

Such increases in land value are immune from recoupment by way of betterment levies or development contributions. In practice, when land is periodically revalued for rating purposes, a small percentage of the increased value is recouped for the community by way of local government rates. However, local government rate revenue is only a very small proportion of total public revenue in Australia.[7] Most of the benefit of the increased land values therefore accrues to landowners. There is currently no mechanism by which the full amount of the increase in land value can be recouped for the public domain. *There is no present solution to this problem.*[8]

Summing up, then, both conceptually and in practice a confused situation currently prevails in respect of the recouping of publicly created land value profits and the related question of community infrastructure funding. In the United Kingdom, against a background littered with failed legislative experiments, the situation in relation to recouping community benefit is described in the literature and by practitioners as a "grey area" that defies resolution. And in Australia, private profiteering in land is institutionalised in a patchwork of only partially effective remedial mechanisms with no identifiable rationale.

Australia approaches the turn of the century with a revived commitment to improving the quality of urban life. There is a recognition of the need to create more equitable and affordable access to housing, transport and community facilities; and on economic, social and environmental grounds there is a recognition of the need to curb the spread of urban settlement into the under-serviced outer suburban wastelands. Yet if initiatives like the Commonwealth's Better Cities Program are to be effective—and politically vindicated—the community's resources will need to be efficiently mustered and efficiently deployed. At present they are being demonstrably eroded by private profiteering calculated to increase and perpetuate social and economic inequality.

Supplementary Notes

1. Australian Institute of Urban Studies, *Second Report of the Task Force on The Price of Land*, Canberra, 1972, p. 37.

2. In Tasmania, for example, the Town and Country Planning Act of 1944 was based on the 1932 English Town and Country Planning Act, as was Victorian legislation of the same year. The Tasmanian Act provided for half of the increase in value to be placed in a betterment fund. The minister who introduced the Bill argued that town planning schemes would "increase the value of properties," and that at least part of the increased value "belonged to the community" (*The Mercury*, 10 November, 1943).

3. The Australian planning system is also flawed in those states where the resolution of planning disputes is conducted adversarily in courts or court-like tribunals. Unlike the inquisitorial or European system, under which an appropriately qualified arbitrator is charged with satisfying himself or herself about the merits of the matter in the public interest (irrespective of the evidence selectively argued by the parties), the adversarial system not only encourages the expensive and time-consuming submission of a great deal of *irrelevant* evidence, manipulation of esoteric procedural rules by contending advocates virtually guarantees that not all the *relevant* information will be brought to bear. While this has no direct bearing upon the issue of land value profits, the cost and formality of the adversarial system tends to deter appeals against development approvals, and continued adherence to the system is symptomatic of institutional apathy.

4. The betterment levy introduced in the ACT in 1971 was originally fixed at 50 percent. It has since been raised to up to 100 percent in circumstances where the landholder's occupancy has been relatively brief. Recently, the rationale of the levy has been clearly affirmed by its application to approvals of "dual occupancy" (where an additional dwelling is allowed on a lot previously occupied by a single dwelling). It should be emphasised that a betterment levy does *not* depend upon land tenure and is equally applicable to freehold and leasehold. The successful implementation of betterment in the ACT is not dependent upon the leasehold tenure under which all land in the ACT is held. Indeed, since land rent was abolished in 1971, the emasculated form of leasehold that now prevails is virtually indistinguishable from freehold.

5. Symtomatic of the ambivalence and confusion that prevails is that the Industry Commission acknowledged that zoning changes could confer "large and instantaneous gains" upon landowners (p. 382) but failed to make any recommendation that such gains should be captured for the community—even though another chapter of the Commission's report affirms that charges on the unimproved value of land are an "important revenue raising instrument" and are "less distorting than other taxes" (pp. 272–276). (Industry Com-

mission, *Taxation and Financial Policy Impacts on Urban Settlement*, Vol. 1, April 1993, AGPS). Even more curious is the express preservation of private windfall profits in Queensland's planning legislation. In 1990, the recently installed Labour government introduced some overdue amendments. Yet it retained the long-standing provision that prevents public acquisition of land in a planning scheme area for purposes such as a public housing estate until *after* the land has been rezoned for urban use. In other words, until after the landowner has reaped the windfall benefit from rezoning—Local Government (Planning and Environment) Act, section 8.1.

6. In the *Standard Hours* case on 21 May, Proceedings p. 7480.

7. Property rates contribute about 50 percent of overall local government revenue, which in turn amounts to less than 5 percent of total public revenue.

8. Typical of current expressions of concern about the funding of urban development is the Australian Local Government Association's inclusion of the following among key issues for local government: "There has been a significant reduction in the past decade of Commonwealth and State funding for infrastructure maintenance, replacement of run-down infrastructure and recurrent funding for services. New ways of financing these requirements have to be found having regard to the principles of equity and efficiency. There is a need for Local Government to increasingly use developer contributions for both physical and social infrastructure in urban areas unless more appropriate and guaranteed capital and recurrent funding is provided by State and Commonwealth Governments." (*Local Government Urban Strategy*, ALGA, Canberra, December 1993, p. 20).

Chapter 3

The Diversion of Investment

Not surprisingly, the profits to be made from land have influenced the direction of investment, and concern about the diversion of savings into land and property at the expense of investment in more productive activities—especially export-oriented manufacturing and servicing—has been voiced by government spokespeople and economic commentators in Australia and elsewhere. Yet there is a dearth of information—or, as an English writer alleges, a conspiratorially contrived "veil of secrecy."[1]

In its research paper entitled *Income Tax and Asset Choice in Australia* (AGPS, Canberra, 1993), the (then) Economic Planning Advisory Council (EPAC) reported that the Australian tax system favoured housing investment and did not recognise many of the external environmental costs caused by private and business activity. After reviewing the incidence of tax at various levels of inflation, and in particular the impact of negative gearing,[2] the paper asserted that "income tax encourages individual Australians to direct their savings towards property rather than new business investment" (p. v). It suggested that remedial measures might include broadening land taxes, the introduction of capital gains tax on the principal place of residence, and the introduction of betterment taxes.

Significantly, however, the EPAC paper did not attempt to quantify the extent of investment in property, and some diverse influences tend to cloud the issue.

Bi-partisan promotion of home ownership throughout the post-war period in Australia has of course created a climate of opinion particularly conducive to the diversion of savings into domestic property; and the diversion of savings into property generally has been stimulated by the permissibility of negative gearing.

American Journal of Economics and Sociology, Vol. 64, No. 5 (November, 2005).
© 2005 American Journal of Economics and Sociology, Inc.

The merits of home ownership as a policy objective, however, are not in contention here—although it can be persuasively argued that home ownership is not readily compatible with the need for mobility in the workforce, or with the need for different kinds of housing at different stages in the typical family life cycle (not to mention the very substantial dollar costs dissipated in real estate commissions and conveyancing, mortgage and valuation fees, which, when coupled with homeowners' expectations of profit upon re-sale, become a built-in contribution to inflation[3]). More to the point is the fact that an eminent social historian, straying into the economic policy arena, does the nation a disservice by insisting that housing is a "productive investment."[4] It might be in a self-contained community. But the diversion of savings into increasingly lavish domestic housing is clearly an unproductive indulgence in a would-be competitive trading nation currently saddled with massive foreign debt.

Even if the application of resources to housing is inextricably embedded in the national psyche, and even if it can be defended on the grounds that it generates employment in the building and construction industries and can be regarded as an accretion to national wealth, a distinction needs to be drawn between houses and the *land* upon which they are erected. No defence of speculative investment in land can be entered on the grounds of employment generation by anyone except perhaps real estate agents on ad valorem commissions and money lenders. An important conclusion can therefore be drawn if the *land* component of housing and land can be shown to be a major speculative component of investment in property. It would then follow that the extent of investment in housing and other property at the expense of more productive investment is at least partly attributable to the scope for profiteering in land detailed in the previous chapter.

The extent of investment in land in Australia has in fact been documented and its significance can therefore be assessed. Statistics compiled by the Melbourne-based Land Values Research Group show that, rising from $42.308 billion in 1986, the total value of real estate sales in Australia (buildings and land) doubled to $87.709 billion at the peak of the real estate boom in 1989. Of this total value of sales, the estimated *land* value component was $61.4 billion, or approximately 70 percent. In fact, the land value component was equivalent to more than 22 percent of national income in 1989.[5]

A further indication of the order of magnitude of property investment at its peak in 1989 can be gained from comparison with sharemarket investment. Sharemarket sales peaked in 1988 at $68.2 billion. Thus, while the precise extent to which savings were actually diverted away from more productive investment can only be surmised, investment in *land* was demonstrably a very significant component of *total* Australian investment in the late 1980s—even more so if it is kept in mind that much of the asset backing of company shares is underpinned by interests in real estate.[6]

That this massive investment in property and land was not sustainable is evidenced by the writing down of property values when the boom collapsed, causing enormous economic dislocation and loss of employment. By June 1992, the Land Values Research Group's data show that some $306 billion (equivalent to one year's national income) had been written off the value of Australian property (mainly in written down *land* value).

Thus, in addition to providing clear evidence of the fact (if not the amount) of the diversion of investment, an analysis of the flow of property investment highlights *the linkage between real estate (especially land) speculation and economic recession in the 1980s*—a linkage reinforced by the historical correlation between earlier property booms and economic recessions.

A third concern of particular interest in the present context is the fact that the foregoing statistics were compiled *by a private organisation*. Neither the Commonwealth Treasury nor the Reserve Bank appears to keep any similar record of capital flows into real estate. As in the United Kingdom,[7] there appears to be an inexplicable missing link in economic policy forecasting data. As the Land Values Research Group publication remarks, if the data the Group assembled had been available to him, the then Treasurer would have been unlikely to have re-introduced negative gearing of residential property investments in August 1987, or to have attributed the flow of funds through the 1980s to a gearing up of capital stock.[8]

Supplementary Notes

1. In *The Power in the Land*, Universe Books, New York, 1983, F. Harrison devotes a chapter to an illuminating historical review of official data collection practices in the United Kingdom and the curious paucity of information about the land market compared with regularly published capital and labour market trends and indices.

2. Offsetting the net cost of borrowing for investment (for example, in housing) against other taxable income.

3. See, for example, J. Kemeny, *The Great Australian Nightmare*, Georgian House, Melbourne, 1983.

4. Hugh Stretton in the preface to the third edition of his *Ideas for Australian Cities*, Transit Australia Publishing, Sydney, 1989; and similarly in various conference papers.

5. Defined as gross domestic product less indirect taxes, subsidies, depreciation allowances and net income payable overseas.

6. The scope for diversion of investment is demonstrable. Yet exemplifying the real or contrived obfuscation prevalent in some quarters is the strange defence of land speculation by A. R. Prest in *The Taxation of Urban Land*, Manchester University Press, 1981. Prest contends that the diversion of investment argument is the "crassest of fallacies" (p. 114), his reasoning being that the proceeds of a sale of land purchased for speculative investment are available to the vendor for investment "at some point in the system" (pp. 130–131). This ignores the fact that (whether in the hands of the vendor or the purchaser) the holding of land in the first instance represents a speculative investment decision in anticipation of an inflationary unearned profit from planning approval. And it assumes that in a speculative boom the vendor will not continue to speculate in land but will "at some point in the system" apply the sale proceeds to a more productive investment.

7. See note 1, above.

8. The Land Values Research Group (Box 2688X, GPO, Melbourne, 3001) published a summary four-page analysis entitled *Anatomy of a Depression* in September 1993. Joint patrons of the Group are Clyde Cameron AO, a former Labour federal minister and Sir Allen Fairhall KBE, a former Liberal federal minister. A more recent Land Values Research Group publication (*The Recovery Myth* by Bryan Kavanagh, 1994) carries the analysis further and demonstrates graphically the remarkably close correlation between unsustainable land booms, fuelled by land speculation at the expense of productive capital investment, and Kondratieff's theory of long wave economic cycles. If the correlation is valid, extrapolation of the graph beyond the latest peak and collapse in 1989–1990 and partial mid-1990s recovery is an ominous portent of depression in the late 1990s.

Chapter 4

The Employment Mirage

WHILE THE ABUSES and incongruities associated with prevailing practice are not unrecognised and, at least in some quarters, are acknowledged with concern, the continuing exploitation of land can nevertheless be plausibly condoned: further "development" can be defended, arguably, on the grounds that it will provide employment. Thus society is confronted with a dilemma. Development may confer inordinate profits on its entrepreneurial proponents and encroach upon the planet's land resources. But for the time being, so the argument runs, uncomfortable doubts must be sublimated and solutions deferred, because ameliorating unemployment is an imperative that must take precedence over all other considerations until economic conditions improve. And, in any case, each new development is only an incremental encroachment.[1]

The argument is plausible, insidiously plausible. Especially if unemployment is indeed only a temporary phenomenon, a consequence of economic recession. Unemployment, after all, is the worst and most destructive form of inequality and unfairness, and the most explicable—even excusable—cause of alienation and crime against property. The urgency of alleviating unemployment must surely take precedence, for the time being, over concerns about proper management of land and the conservation of natural resources. Electoral survival—among politicians at national, state and local level—is perceived to depend on it.

The spectacle of small regional communities, dependent upon exploitative industries, enlisting sympathy for their threatened livelihood, or lured by the perceived bonanza of a "resort" development, is a familiar feature of the national scene. Yet in spite of such parochially populist but ultimately short-sighted special pleading, all the evidence of the 1980s and 1990s shows that socio-economic

American Journal of Economics and Sociology, Vol. 64, No. 5 (November, 2005).
© 2005 American Journal of Economics and Sociology, Inc.

inequality is increasing. The gap between the very rich and the poor is widening, and unemployment is proving intractably difficult to reduce. In Australia, despite high entrepreneurial earnings, the benefits of the so-called resources boom of the early 1980s did not "trickle down." Nor did the profits reaped by the entrepreneurial highfliers in the property boom of the late 1980s. And irreparable environmental damage is a stark reminder of some coastal resort developments that failed.[2]

Broad-based economic salvation through land development is demonstrably a pernicious myth. To the list of consequences that flow from reaping windfall profits from the exploitation of land, yet another deserves to be added: by fostering the delusion that more "development" (including office re-development in the inner city) will remedy unemployment, *land value profiteering stands indicted for effectively diverting attention away from the real causes of unemployment and delaying honest confrontation with them.*

The underlying cause of unemployment is after all not the recent economic recession but Western society's pursuit of a lifestyle that can only be sustained by increasingly skilled employment and capital-intensive, labour-*displacing* technology. The embarrassing paradox is that, while continuing to breed fair-average-quality people, society aspires to a style of living dependent upon production processes *the efficiency of which is measured by the labour that can be dispensed with*—a late 20th-century variation of the Malthusian dilemma. Unless of course the rewards of technologically sophisticated production are equally shared. In which case those with the capacity to occupy themselves in creative alternative pursuits would no doubt welcome release from needless labour. But the twin assumptions involved in this proposition seem regrettably utopian. There is little present prospect of a significant proportion of those earning high incomes in skilled work being willing (or indeed able) to share their work, and even less prospect of their being willing to share their incomes; while the prospect of all those not required to work (or required to work only part-time) being able to occupy themselves creatively seems equally remote.

It is curious, therefore, that, while divergent moral and scientific views are currently being voiced about the capacity of the finite planetary environment—and its finite capacity to absorb waste—to sustain population growth, the question whether full employment, or anything close to it, can be maintained with population growth has not attracted similar attention. For this, land profiteering must share the blame—it has enabled society to take refuge in the plausible assumption that more development, stimulated by the prospect of land value profits, will sufficiently mitigate the situation.

Attempting to alleviate unemployment through continuing encroachment upon the environment ultimately spells ecological disaster. Hoping to alleviate it while simultaneously embracing increasingly sophisticated labour-displacing technology is patently a delusion. In both cases the inescapable inference is that it is not possible to achieve a satisfactory lifestyle in a stable, non-growth society but only by endlessly pursuing growth and borrowing against the future—a lemming-like pursuit of infinite material indulgence in a finite world.[3]

The dilemma seemingly hinges upon the definition of lifestyle. Style of living and standard of living are not necessarily synonymous. If daily evidence of shortcomings and imperfections in government and community services is any indication, virtually all the conceivable improvements to the *standard* of living in Australia lie in the public sector. And virtually all these quality of life improvements are labour dependent and employment sustaining—ranging across the spectrum almost ad infinitum from improved health and education to law enforcement, transport and industrial safety, rehabilitation and training and quarantine and environmental protection, to name but a few of the areas where increased public investment could lead to a happier, safer and more socially responsible community.[4]

The problem of course is the community's traditional reluctance to pay—a reluctance continually nurtured by the exploitation of community cupidity by "low tax" politicians and the popular media and by the seductively easy-fix blandishments of "privatisation." Resolution of the employment dilemma will require a cultural change. And even a shift of emphasis toward the public sector still begs the question whether continuing (physical) growth is necessary and inevitable.

Contemplation of the nature and implications of unemployment is seemingly a digression. But a necessary one. Partly because of the need to expose the spurious condonation of land "development" by those seeking a comfortable panacea—a panacea that those privately profiting from land values increases are only too willing to provide. But also because succeeding chapters will show that, without encroaching interminably upon environmental resources in the pursuit of speculative windfall profits, there are ways of at least making suitable urban land far more affordable than is presently the case for those who wish to establish productive, employment-sustaining enterprises but are deterred by the high price of available land.

Supplementary Notes

1. A variation upon the theme of generating employment at the expense of the natural environment is the encroachment upon public environmental resources (such as parklands) permitted by governments seeking "low tax" solutions to the problem of finding sites for public institutions and for "community" facilities (such as sporting clubs).

2. An example is the appalling desecration of Nelly Bay on Magnetic Island, which commenced in 1989 and remains an indictment of all three major political parties, the Queensland planning appeals system, and all three levels of government (who bankrupted the courageous Nelly Bay woman who challenged them).

3. During the woodchip export controversy dramatised in Australia in early 1995, the logical end result of resource exploitation in an attempt to preserve employment was starkly encapsulated in a banner that read: "No trees *and* no jobs!"

4. For a persuasive analysis of the socially useful, people-intensive employment that could be generated by a shift in lifestyle priorities, see, for example, J. Quiggin writing in the *Canberra Times* of 4.1.94. In a subsequent article in the *Australian Financial Review* of 1.11.94, recalling the hitherto inconceivable ideological and policy shifts that the Australian political scene has witnessed in recent years, Quiggin suggests that obsession with low taxes ought to be the next sacred cow to be killed off. See also Quiggin in *The Age* of 26.12.94. One way or another, the level of unemployment in any community will ultimately depend upon people's willingness to change their lifestyle or pay for other people's employment. The unattractive alternatives to a change in technology-dependent, labour-displacing lifestyle are continuing high unemployment, coupled with a high social welfare payout (the European model); or labour market "reform" to reduce unemployment statistically by enabling the unskilled or insufficiently skilled to negotiate

cut-price or part-time employment with amenable employers (the superficially plausible American model). Both imply the continued existence of a disadvantaged underclass (and the latter assumes that, even at token wages, work will in fact be available). A further unattractive alternative is the Japanese solution, the employment of workers displaced from industry and commerce in a grossly inflated and inefficient public bureaucracy—an extreme version of the Quiggin solution. Massive (non-tariff) import restrictions could of course impact upon unemployment and force a change of lifestyle, though perhaps less acceptably and at the cost of widespread economic distortion.

Chapter 5

Fiscal Masochism

THE WHOLE PHENOMENON of unrecouped land value profits and their consequences and ramifications described in earlier chapters exists in parallel with, and largely detached from, the mechanisms and institutions of mainstream public revenue raising.

In Australia, the principal statutory source of public revenue is the Commonwealth Income Tax Assessment Act. This, together with its associated legislation, is administered by the Australian Taxation Office, which in 1993–1994 collected revenue totaling some $78 billion (at a cost of approximately $1 billion and some 18,000 staff).[1] The Australian tax system is commonly alleged to be one of the most complicated in the world. The Income Tax Assessment Act ran to 126 pages when it was first introduced in 1936. It has been amended every year since. Together with its associated legislation (relating to sales tax, fringe benefits tax assessment, taxation administration and child support assessment) it now runs to a staggering total of 6,715 pages.

Not surprisingly, some 70 percent of the nation's 7.8 million "taxable individuals" now feel obliged to retain tax accountants in order to complete their tax returns. For simple returns this may cost less than $100. But for even a modest income earner with a family, eligible for some deductions, and with some supplementary income from investments, the cost is likely to run to several hundred dollars; while for, say, a self-employed truck driver or machine operator, it may be nearer to $1,000, and for self-employed professionals, small business operators and small manufacturers, several thousand dollars. Such compliance costs are of course exclusive of the time required to assemble all the documentary evidence of income and expenditure and eligible deductions, which, even for an average taxpayer, may be anything from about five to fifteen hours, or even more. *By*

American Journal of Economics and Sociology, Vol. 64, No. 5 (November, 2005).

contrast, in money and time the compliance costs to ratepayers of meeting the revenue needs of local government are nil.

Again not surprisingly, in response to widespread taxpayer frustration the government has announced the establishment of a "Tax Law Improvement Project," which will attempt to rewrite the nation's tax laws, which, in the words of the Assistant Treasurer, are "often very complex, sometimes to the point of being impenetrable for all but the most dedicated expert."[2] The project team comprises some 51 members who will be guided by a consultative committee of 14 members and two observers. The task is expected to take three years. The project is explicitly to improve the existing law, *not* to review tax policy. The first area to be addressed will be the substantiation rules for work expenses, described by the Assistant Treasurer as "an area of notorious difficulty and complexity."[3]

A separate but concurrent review is being undertaken of the record-keeping and other compliance requirements of the fringe benefits tax, which the small business community in particular has condemned as being inordinately burdensome. (FBT contributed a relatively modest 1.8 percent of total tax revenue in 1993–1994.[4])

Over the years the frequency of amendments to the legislation is largely a reflection of continuing endeavours to plug loopholes. Yet new loopholes keep emerging, attributable, for example, to the globalisation of finance, the immediacy of electronic movements of capital and transfer pricing by vertically integrated transnational enterprises, and compounded by increasing sophistication on the part of corporate lawyers and financiers. And at the individual taxpayer level any system of income tax is inherently and very substantially dependent upon voluntary disclosure, and is therefore likely to be characterised by widespread understating of incomes and overstating of deductions. Honest people pay more tax than the less honest and because of the less honest. And, especially in the case of PAYE wage and salary earners (who contribute a major proportion of tax revenue), they do so, resentfully conscious that, for many of their wealthy fellow citizens in the professions and in entrepreneurial activities, there is enormous scope for morally dubious tax minimisation.[5]

Thus the tax system is demonstrably and by common admission defective on three substantial counts: *its absurd complexity, its very high (public and private) compliance costs, and its vulnerability to avoidance and evasion.* To which should probably be added a fourth, *inequity*, because of the extent of avoidance and evasion.

Yet arguably a more serious criticism is that the system is *fundamentally misconceived.* The major revenue source, personal and corporate income taxation, quite literally imposes a penalty on hard work, skill, inventive genius, initiative, enterprise, thrift and self-reliance—all qualities that, in any other context, any community should be anxious to promote and reward. The tax system imposes a disincentive monetary penalty on them all. In recent years, moreover, the prospect of a tax on consuming the (presumably socially desirable) goods and services that the community produces has been actively canvassed—in addition to wholesale taxes, which are effectively a penalty upon their production.

Most incongruous of all of course, particularly in a time of widespread unemployment, is payroll tax—introduced to divert non-essential civilian employment to defence-related employment at the height of World War II, but retained ever since simply as a revenue measure, and subsequently transferred from the Commonwealth to the states (in the course of essentially political inter-governmental bargaining within a federal system). The fact that payroll tax is presently administered (at variable rates) by the states is purely fortuitous, and has no bearing on the fact that it is effectively a component of national revenue raising. While it is less significant (and less avoidable) than income tax as a contribution to total revenue, its now totally indefensible rationale serves to highlight and compound the conceptual ill-logic on which the vast bulk of public revenue raising in Australia is currently founded.

The only significant exceptions to these strictures are local government rates on the occupation and use of land; state land taxes (which in practice, however, are primarily perceived as a tax on wealth rather than a levy on land use); the limited revenue raised from resource rental/royalties levied on petroleum, minerals and forests; and some licensing and service fees, which can be defended as user or beneficiary charges for public services provided.

Capital gains tax, introduced in 1985 on the sale of assets including land (but not the family home or the land on which it stands), is not a separate revenue item. Capital gains are treated as income and taxed accordingly. In some circumstances this may capture—but only coincidentally—some of the windfall gains in land value referred to in earlier chapters.

Supplementary Notes

1. *Annual Report 1993–1994 of the Commissioner of Taxation*, AGPS, Canberra, 1994.
2. The Hon. George Gear in a foreword to *Information Paper No. 1 on the Tax Law Improvement Project*, released by the Commonwealth Treasury in August, 1994.
3. ibid.
4. *Annual Report 1993–1994*, op.cit.
5. A typical device not available to PAYE taxpayers is the service trust by which high income earners such as (some) lawyers and doctors can reduce their tax by spreading their income amongst members of a family trust for secretarial and other services purportedly rendered. Since the trust is legally a separate entity, the diversion of income to it can be inflated because it can legitimately claim a profit margin over and above the actual cost of the services it provides.

Chapter 6

Resourcing Public Revenue

THE PROBLEMS AND issues identified in Chapter 1 and elaborated in the succeeding chapters are demonstrably real. They are not going away. Assuming a will to confront them, to what extent is remedial action possible? Is there any solution, or a complementary mix of solutions, which could resolve the central problem of "unjust enrichment" and all the consequential problems associated with private land value profits—*and* enable revenue for public purposes to be derived without recourse to taxes that penalise labour and enterprise and invite avoidance and evasion?

Some possibilities can be appraised and discarded. Draconian enforcement of town planning schemes could reinforce their integrity and eliminate irresponsible changes in land use, particularly in areas of environmental significance and on the urban fringe. It could be assisted by facilitating citizen-initiated court or tribunal proceedings to compel local government councils to implement and comply with their town plans. But it presupposes an unduly optimistic degree of commitment on the part of their political masters. More importantly, bona fide changes in land use would still have to be made from time to time to meet changing social and economic circumstances. More rigorous town planning would not of itself do anything to prevent windfall profits accruing to landowners.

This is not to say that town planning schemes could not be presented more intelligibly to the citizens whose communities they are intended to benefit. No Australian metropolitan plan has ever inspired as much public interest—and political commitment—as Sir Patrick Abercrombie's 1944 Greater London Plan, which appealed to the beliefs and aspirations of ordinary people and was written in language they could understand. Nor is it to say that there is necessarily anything wrong with developer-led, market-responsive urban

American Journal of Economics and Sociology, Vol. 64, No. 5 (November, 2005).

expansion, provided it takes place within well-conceived strategic planning guidelines. But, whether town planning relies upon broad guidelines or detailed prescriptive controls, the town planning process will remain fundamentally flawed if planning permission confers unearned profits upon landowners.

A betterment levy could solve this problem. A monetary betterment levy (or an equivalent contribution of infrastructure) could capture the full amount of the increase in land value following planning agency approval of development applications or planning scheme variations permitting a more intensive use of land. This would preserve the integrity of town planning schemes, permit open public participation in land use proposals, mitigate the inflationary impact of land value increases, and safeguard environmental resources from speculative development applications generated by an expectation of land value profits.

In other words, a 100 percent betterment levy, or the equivalent in development contributions, would solve many of the problems where the circumstances involved a clear-cut and instantaneous change of land use. There are past and present examples of betterment levies in operation (currently in the ACT, and for several years in NSW in the early 1970s, and overseas notably in Johannesburg and elsewhere in the Transvaal). A betterment levy involves before and after valuations when land use changes take place. There are no major administrative problems, particularly where a system of rating on unimproved land value is already in operation (as in most urban areas in Australia and New Zealand). A 100 percent betterment levy would capture funds for community infrastructure (and for compensating "worsenment"), and to that extent it would relieve the pressure on other forms of revenue raising. It would also reduce the price of land. By eliminating the windfall profit otherwise accruing to the vendor, the price of land would be commensurately reduced. And while any proposal for a betterment levy would attract a Pavlovian response from the development industry, an established and predictable betterment levy system would in fact benefit developers by removing the uncertainty and unpredictability associated with the present practice of negotiating an arbitrary contribution of infrastructure with local government councils.

However, while the logic of a betterment levy is impeccable, a betterment levy does not solve all the problems. There are some circumstances in which unearned land value increases are not amenable to capture by a levy on the difference between before and after valuations. For example, an expectation of a change of land use may evolve over time so that, by the time the formal change is officially approved, the value of the land will have already increased in anticipation. At the time of formal approval the margin between the before valuation and the after valuation will therefore have narrowed and be considerably less. It will not reflect the true increase in land value. A typical case would be in an inner urban area where conversion of low density residential land occupied by detached houses to higher density residential land is likely to be anticipated before a change of use is formally approved by the planning agency. Thus, while a decision approving a change of land use from, say, residential to commercial or industrial may result in an immediate and readily measurable increase in land value, a decision approving increased intensity of an existing land use may only confirm an increase in land value that has already been in prospect over an unspecific time.

Nor, of course, would a betterment levy capture land value increases occurring incrementally over time as a result of population growth and community development. Accordingly, it would not provide funds to meet the converse circumstances and enable landowners to be compensated for gradual, non-specific worsenment occurring over time. And a betterment levy would not discourage landowners from withholding their land from use. Indeed, the prospect of a 100 percent levy might in some circumstances discourage landowners from using (or selling) their land for a more intensive permitted use.

Turning then to land nationalisation, the solution often argued by those who see freehold title as the root cause of land speculation and an insurmountable obstacle in the way of effective town planning. The nationalisation of all land and its subsequent disposal on a leasehold basis for specified purposes subject to an annual rental would certainly ensure that all increases in land value accrued to the community. Whether leasehold tenure would be a guarantee of effective planning is arguable. But the question need not be debated.

Politically and economically the nationalisation of all land in Australia (with or without compensation) is simply not a realistic option.

In England, in pursuance of post-war reconstruction, the 1947 Town and Country Planning Act sought to capture land value increments for the community by nationalising all existing and future development rights attaching to privately-owned land. Compensation was estimated at 300 million pounds sterling. Problems with interpretation and administration, coupled with apprehension about the inflationary impact of such a large payment, delayed implementation of the Act, and the scheme was abandoned by the incoming (Conservative) government.

In Australia, a less ambitious proposal was recommended by the Commission of Inquiry into Land Tenures' First Report in 1973. The Commission avoided the problem of compensation by recommending only that *future* development rights be reserved to the Crown (by analogy with mineral and forestry rights). In other words, it sought to ensure the capture of 100 percent of the betterment attributable to future land use changes. In hindsight, this relatively simple proposition was regrettably overshadowed by a series of complex (and not directly related) recommendations proposing the establishment of public development corporations to control all urban development and re-development. Interest in the Commission's report lapsed after the change of government in 1975, but many passages remain a lucid and professionally competent overview of contemporary issues.[1]

Neither the 1947 Act nor the Land Tenures Report provided for "worsenment," and neither would have prevented the withholding of private land from development (although both envisaged active government intervention in the land market to promote planned re-development). And, while capturing betterment (through the sale of development rights) would have secured substantial funds to finance the provision of public infrastructure and community services, neither would have significantly altered the basis of public revenue raising.

The *only* way to resolve *all* the problems that have been alluded to in the preceding pages can be expressed quite simply. It requires doing, to a greater extent, *what is already being done by all local government councils that levy rates on the unimproved value of land.*

Local government in Australia has historically looked to property rates for the bulk of its revenue. Councils that rate on land typically levy a rate of a few cents in the dollar on the unimproved capital value of land, in effect on its current market value or selling price as assessed periodically by state government valuers. This capital value or notional selling price represents the capitalisation of the rental value of the land if it were rented at an annual rental instead of being purchased outright. *If the rate per dollar value on every parcel of land were increased to an amount equal to its annual rental value,* then, assuming rental values were re-assessed annually, the following consequences would flow:

- the landholder would remain the owner of the land (and any improvements on it);
- the annual rates payable by the landowner to his local government council (as agent of the community) would effectively constitute an annual rental charge for the land;
- every increase in land value would be reflected in the amount of the assessed annual rent; and
- likewise every decrease in land value would be reflected in the amount of the assessed annual rent.

Thus the whole of any increase in land value as a result of land use planning decisions, the advent of new public infrastructure and services or general community growth would be recouped by the council of behalf of the community. No unearned windfall profit would accrue to the landholder. Conversely, landholders would automatically be compensated for the whole of any decrease in land value (for example, to choose a topical illustration, caused by aircraft noise). There would be no uncompensated injurious affection or worsenment. The value—or selling price—of any improvements on the land would not be affected. (But, while the *value* of the land would be its duly assessed value, its *price* or capitalised rental value would be reduced to zero, because no part of the rental value would remain to be capitalised by the landholder if the whole of it were appropriated on behalf of the community).

The further consequences would be:

- *Pressure on the environment would be relieved by the elimination of developmental proposals motivated by the prospect of land value profits.*
- *The integrity of the planning system would be safeguarded and planning decisions could be made on their professional merits.*
- *There could be free and open community participation in land use planning decision making without the risk of information about pending decisions being exploited for speculative private gain.*
- *The speculative withholding of vacant or under-developed land from the market would be discouraged because its rental value would be assessed on the basis of its highest and best permissible use irrespective of its actual use.*
- *National savings would not be diverted away from productive investment by the lure of speculative investment in undeveloped land (or the land component of developed property).*
- *The development industry would cease to be the beneficiary of a hidden land value subsidy, and would be required to rely on the competitive quality of, and market need for, its actual developments.*
- *Access to land by homeseekers and small entrepreneurs would be more affordable because of the elimination of a capitalised purchase price.*
- *And exposing the reality of speculative land "development" at the expense of the environment as a means of employment generation would help to refocus attention on the underlying causes of unemployment.*

But the ramifications of eliminating private profiteering in land extend far beyond these demonstrable benefits. If annual local government property rates were increased to the equivalent of the assessed annual rental value of land, the revenue raised would not only provide ample funds for community infrastructure and services. It would provide *revenue far in excess of the revenue needs of local government.* In which case it could contribute to the revenue needs of other levels of government, and revenue raised from other sources could be correspondingly reduced. Particularly if other means of revenue raising were seen to penalise thrift and enterprise, involve high compliance costs and induce a misallocation of resources.

The implications for public revenue raising therefore deserve to be further explored.

One of the most comprehensive reviews of revenue raising in Australia in recent years was that undertaken on behalf of the nation's largest local government authority, the Brisbane City Council, by the Lord Mayor's Committee of Inquiry into Valuation and Rating, which produced an exhaustive two-volume report in September 1989. Given the Committee's wide-ranging terms of reference and its approach to them, reference in some detail is instructive.

The Committee adopted as its twin, over-riding objectives the pursuit of equity and efficiency. Over the course of two and a half years it reviewed the philosophy and principles of taxation. It compiled a matrix of all the desiderata against which revenue raising alternatives could be tested. Having regard to the benefit principle, the ability-to-pay principle and the notion of universality of contribution, it proceeded to assess possible forms of revenue raising in terms of revenue potential, economy of collection, tax effectiveness, market efficiency, policy effectiveness, visibility, intelligibility, autonomy and relationship to benefit.

In the course of its deliberations the Committee became firmly persuaded that the benefit principle rather than ability-to-pay (sometimes referred to as the highwayman's approach to revenue raising) was the most equitable and rational basis of taxation. Thus, in the words of its report, "the Committee came to the fundamental conclusion that, in seeking to recover the cost of the works and services it provided, a revenue raising authority should—as far as possible—charge the beneficiaries or users of such works and services to the extent that such works and services and their beneficiaries or users could be distinguished and were identified; and that, where works and services were not, or could not be, separately identified and specifically charged for, their cost should be recovered by some form of basic general charge which should nevertheless as far as possible reflect the benefit principle."

In order to satisfy itself about the most appropriate basic general charge, the Committee then evaluated, against its adopted criteria, poll taxes, taxes on income and on sales, taxes on land value and on improved property value and licence fees (as well as the scope for local government trading enterprises and joint ventures). It came to the unanimous conclusion that rating on the unimproved value of land was the most efficient and equitable general revenue base for Brisbane, and, significantly, expressed the view that, "in principle, the unimproved value of land is a logical and appropriate basis for revenue raising *irrespective of the level of government"* (emphasis added).

In coming to this conclusion, the Committee noted, amongst other advantages, that a tax on land value was virtually impossible to evade; that it represented a contribution by every member of the community either directly as a property owner or indirectly by way of rent or board; that its administration was simple and inexpensive; and that its compliance costs for citizens were minimal. It also observed that a land value tax was an effective mechanism for achieving a city's town planning objectives in that it induced the development of land for its best and most intensive permissible use.

The Committee was impressed by the fact that, since land was a commodity in fixed supply, a charge levied at the same percentage rate on all land users would not affect the free market allocation of resources and could not be passed on. Moreover, since the rental value of land in a competitive market, when capitalised, gave land its capital value, to the extent that the community captured some of the rental value of land by way of tax, a land value tax would operate to depress the price of land. While a tax on land could be levied either upon its unimproved capital value (in accordance with past practice) or upon its annual rental value, the Committee observed that theoretically the latter basis more correctly reflected the recouping by the community of part of the land's rental value.

Like a poll tax (but without its blatantly regressive and inequitable impact), a tax on unimproved land value complied with the notion of universal contribution; and it straddled the ability-to-pay and benefit principles of taxation. Ownership of valuable land was arguably evidence of capacity to pay (if not ability, when heavily mortgaged), and, while not specifically conceived as a wealth tax, it bore most heavily on those who had the capacity to own the most valuable land. It therefore automatically performed a redistributive function. At the same time, owners of land were beneficiaries of its natural attributes and the public works and services provided to it, as well as the less tangible but nevertheless real benefits of membership of a cohesive, organised and mutually supportive community.

The Brisbane inquiry was required to review *modes* of revenue raising. It was not concerned with the *amount* of revenue raised, and in the course of evaluating modes of revenue raising the Committee assumed a revenue-neutral end result. Thus it made no recommendations about the rate in the dollar value of land that should be levied, or could be levied. It therefore made no attempt to quantify the *potential* revenue that could be raised by rating on land value. Australian local government receives a subvention from the national government's tax revenue and is therefore not wholly dependent upon revenue from rates or from other local fees and charges. Thus the question of a tolerance or saturation level in relation to rating revenue was not in issue. (Local government ratepayers are also national government taxpayers, and any notional balancing of rate revenue and tax revenue is therefore a matter of political judgement.)

Historically, rates levied on land have raised only a small proportion of the revenue that *could* be raised if the annual rate on the capital value of a parcel of land were equal to the annual rental value of the land. In the absence of any actual assessment of annual rental values, an indication of how small the present proportion is can be arrived at by deriving approximate annual rental values by assuming a capitalisation rate and working back from assessed unimproved *capital* values (which are how land valuations are currently expressed). Depending on the capitalisation rate adopted, typical figures for Brisbane suggest that actual rate revenue presently derived from land is somewhere around 15 percent of the potential revenue that could be raised if the rate were equivalent to the annual rental value.

Some idea of the revenue potential Australia-wide of capturing the annual rental value of land can be gained from the fact that a conservative estimate of the present capital value of all land in Australia is about $450 billion. Depending on the capitalisation rate adopted, this suggests that the presently uncollected annual rental revenue in Australia could be something approaching $40 billion—clearly sufficient to allow for the elimination or substantial reduction of some existing taxes.[2] (For comparison, income tax revenue in 1993–1994 was $67.6 billion and sales tax revenue was $10.4 billion. Payroll tax receipts for all states totaled $6.04 billion.)

Historically, the question of whether land rental could suffice to meet the total revenue needs of modern government has been the subject of considerable theorising. Some early theorists suggested that it would provide *more* than enough. Given that total public revenue raised in Australia by all governments from all sources in 1993–1994 was in the order of $148 billion, this seems unlikely. There are no present means of knowing. There are too many inter-related variables that are not presently quantified (but that could be quantified).

For example, it would be interesting to know the savings in compliance costs. Administering the present tax system costs the Australian Tax Office about $1 billion a year and requires a staff of nearly 18,000. If land rental were a major source of public revenue, public sector compliance costs would be considerably less, while for the private sector the cost of compliance with the land rental component of its contribution to revenue would literally be reduced to zero. The latter would be a not insignificant benefit to the private sector, but neither of these savings has any direct bearing on potential revenue— although the former would marginally reduce the amount of revenue needed to be raised.

More significantly, no revenue would be lost through evasion (by way of cash transactions, barter, dishonesty or non-compliance), and no revenue would be lost by way of legitimate but difficult to counter loopholes and avoidance techniques (such as transfer pricing by internationally-based corporations). Even so, for any given revenue target, avoiding these losses would only reduce the tax burden on those upon whom the tax burden presently falls—a welcome enough and by no means insignificant benefit, but it would not affect the extent to which land rental revenue would be able to meet total revenue needs.

It can be argued, however, that following the introduction of land rental and the concurrent abolition or reduction of taxes that currently

penalise labour and enterprise, increased business activity and productivity would increase demand for land and increase its rental value
and therefore public revenue. It is also at least arguable that social
welfare demands upon public revenue would be less because more
affordable access to land would be likely to generate employment
and increase self-dependence. (And if income taxation ceased to be
the main revenue source, there would be no need to impose embarrassing supplementary earning limits upon welfare recipients.)

However, in the absence of more precise information—and it
should be emphasised that nothing hinges upon the accuracy of what
can at best only be indicative approximations[3]—pursuing the question of whether land rental alone could meet total public revenue
needs is unrealistic. It is also unnecessary. Every government in its
wisdom or otherwise is entitled, as a matter of social (or environmental) policy, to levy excise and customs duties and discriminatory
sumptuary taxes (for example, on alcohol, tobacco and petrol). And
as the Brisbane report emphasises, on the grounds of equity
governments should also recoup revenue as far as possible from
user charges where the beneficiaries of public services can be identified and appropriately charged[4] (subject always to an acceptable
minimum standard of essential services being available to all members
of the community). In other words, the notion of land rental sufficing as the sole source of public revenue or "single tax" is inapt and
misconceived.

To meet government expenditure, the alternatives to raising
revenue from user charges and from land and other natural resources
rental are: borrowing; levying taxes on human resources (on income
and capital); charges upon goods, and upon the consumption of
goods—and printing money. What can be said with conviction—
notwithstanding the present difficulties in the way of estimating the
precise proportion—is that *recouping the full annual rental of land,
together with user charges for public services, could, at the very least,
very substantially reduce reliance upon these other options* (particularly those that discourage productive activity and encourage evasion).

Some of course would prefer to view it the other way round and
argue that the extent to which public expenditure is confined to
resource rental revenue (and not supplemented by borrowing or

inflation) is a valid measure of financial responsibility. In this regard it should perhaps be added that, unlike other taxes, land value rental is a source of revenue that cannot be arbitrarily increased at the whim of governments. At any given time the rental value of a parcel of land is fixed. It is a precisely assessed amount peculiar to that parcel at that time.

In 1984 the then Commonwealth Treasurer, and in 1993 the then Leader of the Opposition, advocated the introduction of a consumption tax on goods and services in order to fund a reduction of income and company taxes. Another justification advanced for a goods and services tax is that it would ensure less tax avoidance by the wealthy. Land rental would achieve both objectives. But, unlike a goods and services tax, it would not be regressive. It would not penalise the production and sale of socially worthwhile goods and services. And it would not be inflationary. Indeed, it would eliminate the capital price of land. It would be a "consumption tax" on *land*, the most natural and inherently justifiable subject of a consumption charge.

Timing the introduction of annual land rental (and the simultaneous reduction of other revenue taxes or charges) would be the most difficult practical question.

To the extent that it is meaningful to refer to average rate levies among the hundreds of Australian local government councils that presently levy rates on unimproved land value, it can be assumed that probably something in the order of about 15 percent of the annual rental value of land is currently being recouped, relatively painlessly, by local government. Putting it another way, about 15 percent of the annual rental value of land is being collected on behalf of the community (plus, in the case of a small minority of landowners, an additional amount by way of state land taxes). Both local government rates and state land taxes tend to marginally depress the price (but not the value) of land. But if the full 100 percent of the annual rental value were to be collected at one stroke, the selling price of all land would be reduced to zero, with unacceptably dire consequences for anyone who had recently purchased land in good faith for whatever purpose (including speculation). And the impact would be only relatively less traumatic for a recent purchaser of a developed property if the land component of his purchase price were likewise reduced to zero overnight. For the purpose of using property as a security, for example, the value of undeveloped land, or of the land component of developed property, would be extinguished.

There are of course many circumstances in which people's investments can be adversely affected adventitiously and unavoidably (for example, by the diversion of highways away from shops or service stations previously relying on passing trade; or by the advent of new technology). Nevertheless, while long-time landowners would suffer no disadvantage and would enjoy the simultaneous relief from other taxes, the consequences for some recent purchasers of immediately forgoing 100 percent of the annual rental value of their land could be unconscionable. The introduction of full annual land value rental would therefore need to be spread over perhaps up to 10 years (during which time any anomalies arising in particular circumstances in the course of balancing the increasing incidence of charges on land and the declining incidence of other taxes and charges could also be adjusted).

Another practical question (which arises now but to a lesser degree) is that of the impact of increased land rental charges upon property owners who are "asset-rich but income-poor" (and would therefore derive little or no compensating advantage from the elimination or reduction of income tax). The problem arises now in the case of pensioners or retired people living in urban locations that have become increasingly valuable over the course of time (or because of zoning changes foreshadowing more intensive land use). It may also arise in cases of special hardship or sudden unemployment. The solution lies in the fact that land rental is a levy on land and not on persons. It can therefore be deferred and remain, very properly, a charge on the land (until the property is sold, transferred by inheritance, or used for a more valuable purpose permitted by re-zoning).

These questions are further discussed in subsequent chapters. Summing up to this point, some reiteration may be excusable: in the form of rates on the capitalised rental value, *land value rental is already being recouped to some degree by Australian local government (and has been recouped for nearly 100 years)*. There are no insurmountable practical obstacles in the way of gradually recouping it in full—not as the sole but as the most equitable and efficient basic source of public revenue—*and simultaneously realising the very substantial social, economic and environmental benefits identified earlier in this chapter.*

Supplementary Notes

1. The Commission's report reviews the evolution of land law in Australia (at pp. 39 et seq.), noting that terms such as "freehold" and "leasehold" tend to reflect philosophical differences rather than definitive distinctions in law, and that all landowners in Australia are, strictly, tenants of the Crown. Given the identity of the commissioners (Judge Rae Else-Mitchell of the Supreme Court of NSW; Russell Mathews, Professor of Accounting and Public Finance at the Australian National University; and Mr. Gerardus Dusseldorp, Chairman of Lend Lease Corporation Limited) and the unanimity of their findings, what the report says about the development industry's alleged need for "incentives" is pertinent. "Redevelopment initiatives should not depend on the prospect of private capital gains arising out of changes in use. If redevelopment is unprofitable in the absence of such gains, it is premature and it is against the public interest to permit it to take place" (p. 13). Again (at p. 24): "It is sometimes argued that, if the whole of the development value is appropriated by the Crown, private initiatives to undertake development will be destroyed with adverse consequences for the public interest. This argument seems to us to confuse initiatives relating to land dealing with initiatives relating to the land development process . . . the developer will still make his profit, but this will be earned from the development process itself and will not include any increment in value resulting from the change in land use."

Little has changed over 20 years. Reporting in 1973, the Commission observed that "millions of dollars are won or lost by a decision of an elected local governing council or by the stroke of a planner's pen. Those millions of dollars come from the collective pockets of the community and, especially in the case of outer suburban land, from the pockets of those groups in the community least able to pay—young couples purchasing their first homes . . . In Australia, town planning has long been treated with cynicism, no doubt because of the manner in which it has been conducted. Wherever there is the prospect of private profit from planning decisions two results follow: planning is necessarily performed in secret, and there is a suspicion of manipulation for private ends. Pressures will be exerted to achieve planning changes which are profitable to individual landowners rather than desirable in the public interest. Where a decision is necessarily rather arbitrary, such as in drawing a boundary between the urban area and its rural hinterland, the pressures become almost irresistible . . . But if the expectation of private gain from land use decisions is removed the position wholly changes. No longer will it be to the advantage of the individual landowner to have his land rezoned; no longer will pressure to that end be exerted by him. Because no private profit can be made the need for planning secrecy will disappear. Plans should be the object of public discussion at all stages of formulation. Planning decisions should be made on the basis of serving public needs rather than on the basis of accommodating private interests" (p. 18).

2. The estimate of the total capital value of land in Australia has been supplied by the Melbourne-based Land Values Research Group. Strictly speaking, this global estimate is the capitalisation of the *uncollected* annual rental value, since some of the rental value has already been collected via local government rates and state land taxes and the residual capitalised value (available from public records) has been correspondingly reduced. The total *potential* annual rental revenue (i.e., the total of collected and uncollected rental revenue) is therefore probably something over $50 billion. (Based on current average yields, a capitalisation rate of between 8 and 9 percent has been adopted for the purpose of deriving annual rent from capital values.)

3. Apart from the problem of tracing the revenue source of inter-governmental transfer payments, any objective disaggregation of Australian public revenue sources is difficult because of inter-state variations and variations among local governments in recouping utility costs (for example, for water and sewerage) partly by way of user charges and partly by way of property rates. A further difficulty is the classification of stamp duty, a major source of state revenue, which is arguably a property-related revenue tax (and one that in practice tends to be regressive).

4. For example, user charges on the *consumption* of water as distinct from the *availability* of reticulated water, which is properly a component of land value.

Chapter 7

Underpinning a Global Morality

FOR THE WRITER, some of the issues discussed in the preceding chapters were seen in sharper focus in the course of a visit to Russia in late 1993.

In the volatile transitional circumstances prevailing in the former Soviet Union, any Western observer who explores land administration practices must be prepared to grapple with a mixture of familiar mechanisms and mind-blowing incongruities. In a society culturally unfamiliar with land title registration and property valuation (except, incredibly, on a flat-rate unit area basis), there are curious voids in basic conceptual awareness. About the very concept of property, for example, and the fundamental distinction between land and improvements and about the normal and natural differences between urban and rural land values. Yields from some arbitrarily implemented property taxes have been so trivial that some local governments have refused to collect them. Widespread confusion has prevailed about the meaning and implications of privatisation, coupled with absurd incongruities in the availability and pricing of goods and services. Some lucky tenants of Moscow apartments acquired ownership for the equivalent of a mere few dollars. Many of the incongruities appear to reflect the failure of a misdirected command economy rather than public ownership per se, and the pursuit of "privatisation" as a perceived panacea appears to have obscured appreciation of the fact that transition from a command economy to a market-responsive economy may not necessarily require wholesale privatisation.

How far and how fast the Russians move in the direction of land and fiscal reform remains to be seen. In late 1993, it was evident that there was considerable apprehension that Western-style capitalism, notwithstanding efforts over time to temper its excesses, appeared to have no philosophical motivation other than the pursuit of profit and

American Journal of Economics and Sociology, Vol. 64, No. 5 (November, 2005).
© 2005 American Journal of Economics and Sociology, Inc.

self-interest, and that complex revenue raising mechanisms that taxed labour and enterprise appeared to put a premium on evasion and deceit. On the other hand, there was widespread recognition that the demise of the old order provided Russia with a unique opportunity for profound political, economic and philosophical change.

Discussions with senior officers of Gostroi, the Russian ministry of town planning and construction, and with representatives of the Union of Russian Cities, were focused on ways and means of providing for private possession and use of land. There was considerable support for the notion of exclusive private possession of land, in perpetuity if need be, coupled with absolute private ownership of buildings and other improvements erected on land, subject, however, to payment to the community of an annually assessed charge or land rent determined by public valuers. Despite difficulties in conceptualising economic rent and its annual re-assessment, and the practical problems posed by inadequate cadastral maps and a dearth of experienced valuers, there were expressions of strong support for providing for private possession of land on this basis. The pervasive influence of Tolstoy, an ardent proponent of land reform, was apparent. While for all practical purposes a private land market along these lines would be no different from a land market in Western societies, it would nevertheless be characterised by one fundamental distinction: it would acknowledge that land—as distinct from man-made improvements on it—was a finite natural resource that logically and morally belonged ultimately to the community. Not surprisingly, this distinction appeared to evoke a sympathetic response among Russians apprehensive about privatisation of their national birthright in the pursuit of the holy grail of foreign capital investment.

Representatives of local government competing for growth and industrial development appeared to be impressed by the fact that eliminating the capital price of land—coupled with diminution of other forms of taxation—would not only benefit homeseekers and farmers. It would enable entrepreneurs to establish their own small businesses and help to bring about the phasing out of the "kiosk economy"—the ubiquitous proliferation of temporary stalls in the streets and subways. There was likewise recognition that an effective and genuinely participatory town planning system and a land value rental system could be mutually reinforcing. Town planning controls would be a primary determinant of assessed land value, while land value rental would discourage speculative withholding of land from its planned use, as well as ensuring the availability of funds for community infrastructure. And the level of rent offered—initially at government auctions and subsequently in the market—would provide planners with an indication of the demand for various categories of land uses.[1] One gained the impression, moreover, that paying rent to the community would be more palatable to the Russian psyche than paying "taxes" to the "state."

A senior presidential policy aide indicated his personal commitment to imposing charges on land. However, the influence of perceived "rationalists" among World Bank economists advising the President was viewed with suspicion, the feeling being that the President would be dissuaded from any departure from conventional Western land disposal practices—even though, ironically, a land value rental system that acknowledged the ultimate "ownership" of land by the Russian people would obviate the need to limit or discriminate against the exclusive *possession* of land by foreign investors.

Capturing the full annual rental value of land implies, of course, the simultaneous elimination of equivalent central government taxes and inter-governmental agreement about the re-apportionment of public revenue. In Russia this has implications for the status of some of the large cities, which have been contemplating substantial fiscal autonomy in relation to land. Some have even aspired to "republic" status. Time will tell.

What visiting Russia confirmed was the *latent universality of the concept of raising public revenue primarily from land*. Recognition of land as a community resource would provide any society with a unifying moral basis—a moral basis conspicuously absent in the West and ignored by the Stalinist practitioners of Marxism, yet equally capable of underpinning a market-oriented economic system or a highly regulated one.[2] Indeed, distinguishing between land as a finite natural resource and man-made commodities offers a *tangible and readily comprehensible basis for environmental conservation on a global scale*—in lieu of exhortations and lamentations, which can never prevail against ever-increasing exploitation generated by the lure of land value profits.[3]

What is profoundly uncomfortable to a Western observer is the impression that, untrammelled by long-entrenched assumptions about the sanctity and rectitude of private land "ownership," the societies emerging from communist tyranny may conceivably be more disposed to move toward a more equitable and morally sustainable society based on land and taxation reform than the nations of the West. In former communist countries, a change from state ownership to a system under which, subject to payment of an annual rental, citizens obtained exclusive permanent possession of land for their occupation and use is likely to be regarded as a progressive enlargement of civic rights and, as a means of raising public revenue, conceptually fair and natural. By contrast, reflecting their cultural dilemma about the special nature of land and their ambivalence about capturing land value increases—coupled with the fine dividing line between legitimate profitmaking, the theoretical mainspring of capitalism, and the unscrupulous greed and self-interest to which capitalism in practice is inherently vulnerable—Western societies have resorted to piecemeal measures that leave the basic problem unresolved but mindlessly accepted and institutionalised. To a Queenslander conscious of the continuing vulnerability of his state's south-eastern corner to developer-driven exploitation in the pursuit of land value profits, there was piquant irony in having contributed to the Russian debate.

Supplementary Notes

1. A land market would operate in essentially the same way as it operates in Western societies. Any premium offered to the possessor of land by way of an inducement to transfer possession would be recorded and taken into account in re-assessing the annual land value rental in the same way that the sale price in Western societies is required by law to be disclosed so that it can be taken into account in re-assessing the capitalised value thereafter for valuation and rating purposes.

2. Marx's writings are notoriously ambiguous, but in Book 3 of *Das Kapital* he appears to endorse the collection of economic rent. The subsequent course of Marxism is discussed hereunder in the concluding chapters.

3. In Australia, recognition of the special status of land, coupled with an obligation upon occupiers of land to pay an annual rent to the community, would not in itself resolve all the questions arising from the High Court decision in the Mabo land titles case. It would, however, help to lay to rest the *terra nullius* myth and contribute to national reconciliation by taking some of the emotional heat out of the "land rights" debate. It would be a unifying influence underpinning multiculturalism in Australia, which in microcosm represents the world community—the ultimate "owner" of the planet's land resources.

Chapter 8

The Essential Requirements

ADOPTING ANNUAL LAND rental values as the primary source of public revenue requires acceptance of one fundamental pre-condition: namely, recognition that land is a finite resource provided by nature and therefore distinguishable from all man-made goods, structures and services. *Plus* an acknowledgement that individual persons who use or occupy this resource owe an obligation to the wider global community upon whom nature has bestowed it (which for practical administrative purposes means an obligation to nation-states or other recognised community groupings).

Given acceptance of this fundamental pre-condition, there are really only three basic institutional requirements:

- There must exist a public land planning and administration authority responsible for planning and determining the use of all land; and, at any given time, the permissible or intended use of all land must be indicated on publicly available cadastral planning maps and supporting documents.
- There must be a public register or record of all landholding.
- There must be a public land valuation authority—preferably separate from and independent of the land planning and public revenue agencies—capable of assessing and maintaining an up-to-date record of the annual rental value of all parcels of land.

While these are the essential requirements, certain additional desiderata should perhaps be recorded. Thus it would be desirable to explicitly acknowledge the right of all citizens (including corporate bodies) to enjoy the secure and exclusive occupation and use of land, subject to compliance with the town planning controls applicable to it and acceptance of an obligation to pay its assessed annual rental value to the community as represented by the government; and likewise to

American Journal of Economics and Sociology, Vol. 64, No. 5 (November, 2005).
© 2005 American Journal of Economics and Sociology, Inc.

explicitly acknowledge the right of every lawful occupier of land to own, and profit from, improvements lawfully erected on the land, and be compensated in full for the value of any such improvements in the event of the land being required for a public purpose.[1]

It would be desirable to have in place simple, non-legalistic appeals systems to enable citizens to have land use decisions reconsidered and the official assessment of the annual rental value of their land reviewed; and to resolve disputes about the market value of the improvements if their land is required for a public purpose.

It would further be desirable (as indicated in Chapter 6) to make express provision for the deferment of the rental obligation in cases of hardship, more particularly in circumstances where a planned upgrading of permissible land use results in a substantial increase in the assessed annual rent. And generally, along with the promulgation of civic rights and responsibilities, it would be desirable to promote greater public awareness and understanding of land planning and property valuation processes and procedures and their relationship to public revenue raising.

In most Western societies the essential institutional requirements already exist or can readily be established, but the fundamental conceptual recognition of the status of land is lacking. By contrast, in many developing societies and in communist or formerly communist societies the institutional mechanisms may presently be inadequate, whereas the fundamental conceptual pre-condition is (or up till now has been) acknowledged in some degree, either in tribal custom or in the state ownership of all land and property. Remedying their institutional shortcomings may be easier than persuading Western societies to recognise the special status of land.

Certainly, the maintenance of up-to-date valuations is critically important. This was not understood in Canberra. At the time of federation the framers of the Australian Constitution were keenly aware of the need to prevent land speculation. Thus section 125 provides that the territory for the seat of government "shall be vested in and belong to the Commonwealth." In the subsequent administration of early Canberra's leasehold tenure, however, it was decided that land rentals should be re-assessed only at 20-year intervals. When rentals were re-assessed after the rapid post-war growth of Canberra, the rental increases were so great that popular opposition caused the government misguidedly to abolish the land rental system. Landholders retained the benefit of huge increases in the value of their land, and the scope for Canberra to become substantially self-funding (like the early post-war English new towns) was lost.

Frequent re-valuations are necessary to ensure that rental values reflect changes in economic circumstances as well as community growth. Thus assessed annual rentals should rise correspondingly in economic booms, and be reduced promptly in conformity with economic decline (for example, in the advent of bad seasons, poor harvests, a decline in export prices or a decline in the tourist trade). Frequent re-valuations avoid public perception of unconscionably sudden and steep increases in assessed rentals.

In the United Kingdom the failure to maintain up-to-date property valuations (coupled with the absence of a firm tradition of separately valuing *unimproved* land) led to the Thatcher government's abortive attempt to introduce a blatantly regressive poll tax in lieu of property taxes.

Whether government departments and authorities should—at least notionally—be liable for paying to the public treasury the annual rental value of land they occupy (and for offsetting the impact of any developments they undertake), is a question of administrative philosophy. Government departments and authorities may well use land more efficiently if they are reminded of its value.

Supplementary Notes

1. Whether any residential or citizenship qualifications or any quantitative limits on landholding should apply are policy questions for national governments. If all land value profits accrued to the community, rational opposition to "foreign ownership" would be difficult to sustain.

Chapter 9

Impediments and Counter-Arguments

BEFORE ATTEMPTING TO identify the kinds of opposition that a commitment to a land value rental regime might attract, it may be worth
reiterating (a) that land value rental could only be fully implemented
over a period of years in Western societies; (b) that, as a public
revenue raising mechanism, it is revenue-neutral and does not imply
any variation in the quantum of public revenue raised; and (c) that
it is politically and ideologically neutral and equally adaptable to both
capitalist and socialist economic systems.

One source of opposition may certainly be anticipated. Land value
rental would be strongly opposed by anyone deriving—or hoping to
derive—a significant income from speculative investment in land, or
from the mere fact of landholding. Those with a vested interest in
profiting from land would be vocal and influential and, if confirmation were needed, the strength and virulence of their opposition
would be a measure of the profits that are currently being made from
landholding. Overt defence of profiteering would be unlikely. Instead,
inspired opposition would more likely be couched in terms calculated to evoke the spectre of "land nationalisation" in the minds of
every property owner, however humble. Indeed, especially the
humble. Abolishing the private appropriation of land value increases
would be portrayed as "confiscation"; and the development industry
would sound dire warnings about removing the "incentive" to
"develop," and the alleged implications of this for employment. There
would be emotive but erroneous evocations of "leasehold."[1] Probably even of "socialism" (or worse)—even though land monopolisation is the antithesis of individualism and free enterprise and
eliminating unproductive land speculation would make access to land
more affordable for bona fide industry and commerce.

While land value rental would enable all income earners (including land speculators) to be relieved wholly or substantially of the

American Journal of Economics and Sociology, Vol. 64, No. 5 (November, 2005).
© 2005 American Journal of Economics and Sociology, Inc.

burden of income taxation levied on their labour, enterprise or investment income, a conspiracy to distort the reality of land value rental could nevertheless exploit initial apprehension among all landholders and delay their assimilation and acceptance of some of the consequential features of a land value rental regime.

On the face of it, for example, it could be disconcerting to realise that landholders would receive no selling price (other than any premium that a transferee might offer as an inducement) when they transferred ownership of their land—even though they would not have to pay any purchase price to procure alternative land. They would of course be able to sell the improvements on their land, and they would have to buy the improvements on any other land they chose to acquire. The value of real estate as a security for borrowing would likewise be confined to the value of the improvements. But, where the borrowing was for the purpose of acquiring other real estate, the borrowing requirement would be similarly reduced. These are the necessary consequences of accepting the logically unassailable distinction between unimproved land (provided by nature) and negotiable man-made improvements erected on it. However, if the transition to recouping the total annual rental value of all land for the community were to take place incrementally over a period of years, assimilating the impact of these changes would not be a significant problem.

Superficially it might be thought that farmers and pastoralists holding substantial areas of land would be disadvantaged. This is demonstrably not so. Land value rental is only concerned with the assessed market value of parcels of land regardless of their size. Theoretically, farmers or anyone else subject to seasonal fluctuations would in fact be positively advantaged by paying annually adjusted land rent instead of fixed interest instalments on their land purchase price.

In Australia, attitudes to land value rental are likely to be coloured by experience of "land tax," the history of which needs to be briefly recounted. The six states introduced land taxes, starting with South Australia in 1884 and finally with Queensland in 1915. The Commonwealth entered the field in 1910, but vacated it in 1952, since when land tax has continued to be levied by the states on major landholders at varying rates and subject to varying exemptions and commencement thresholds. Enthusiasm for land reform around the turn of the century had been reflected, for example, in the adoption of unimproved land value for municipal rating and for state land taxes by several states prior to federation. It was also reflected in the vesting of ownership of the territory for the seat of government in the infant Commonwealth. However, by the time Commonwealth land tax was introduced in 1910, land tax was viewed primarily as a revenue source and wealth tax, a view reinforced by its implementation by the Commonwealth and some of the states at progressive rates of incidence.

As a consequence of this departure from principle, present state land taxes are a discriminatory levy upon a minority of individual and corporate landholders. They are literally a tax, an arbitrarily assessed revenue raising mechanism with no other discernible rationale. They are not in any sense a land value charge for the occupation and use of the community's land resources. Opposition to present state land taxes is therefore well-founded, but their well-warranted unpopularity may unfortunately tend to cloud recognition of the validity of the quite separate and distinct concept of land value or community resource rental.

At first sight some plausible opposition could also focus on the circumstances of those in the category of "asset-rich but income-poor," typically retired people whose properties in inner urban areas have become increasingly valuable by virtue of their location or re-zoning. Any advantage such people would derive from a reduction in income tax would be likely to be outweighed by the land value rent to which they would be subject. This problem has been alluded to earlier. It already exists in the case of municipal rates and can be resolved in the same way. Local government councils typically offer pensioner rate remissions, or in some cases deferment. Deferment is the logical and proper answer. Rates are a charge on land and can properly be deferred until the land is used for a more intensive purpose or until ownership changes by sale or inheritance. Remission, on the other hand, is morally and logically unwarranted. Society has no obligation to present transferees or legatees with valuable properties unencumbered because the revenue foregone by remission has been contributed by the remainder of the rate-paying community—including ratepayers who, for reasons of temporary hardship, may be in far less comfortable circumstances than pensioners enjoying remission.[2]

Tax accountants and tax lawyers of course would not be enthusiastic about land value rental if it gradually replaced personal and corporate income tax as a major source of public revenue. And considerably fewer staff would be required in the Taxation Office. The professional status of valuers, on the other hand, would tend to increase, with some justification.

At the other end of the spectrum it may be that there are some who would expect too much. Apart from eliminating speculative windfall profits and mitigating inequality of wealth derived solely from the possession of land, land value rental is ideologically neutral. It is not a vehicle for equalising or redistributing wealth acquired through the socially acceptable exercise of labour, skill or inventive genius— although it would ensure that any claims upon the community's land resources as a result of the subsequent expenditure of such wealth were subject to the payment of a commensurate rental to the community.

In the course of their activities the processors and distributors of information in the burgeoning "information society" may make relatively modest claims on the community's land resources. Many professional people and others in the "brain-power" industries may likewise have only modest land requirements. As, indeed, would a successful artist in a garret. Assuming a competitive marketplace and assuming also that the airwaves were, like land, treated as a natural community resource, if society considered the financial rewards of such people were nevertheless excessive, it would need to look to other ways of containing them. Likewise if the possession of wealth were perceived to confer inordinate political power. But the fact that some people with special skills earn high incomes is not a reason for *not* requiring all people to compensate the community for the land resources they choose to use or occupy in the course of their vocations (or in the subsequent exercise of their wealth).

Land value rental would certainly equalise opportunity by ensuring more affordable access to land, and it would mitigate *unearned* inequality of wealth. But it is not a vehicle for the pursuit of absolute equality—if that were ever a realistic goal—or for taxing wealth per se. The latter after all is a misconception. If wealth creation is an accepted societal goal, then income and capital taxes on wealth acquired by socially acceptable means are logically indefensible. They can be plausibly justified by notions of ameliorating inequality and the assumption that the wealthy have a greater capacity to pay. But the notion of ameliorating inequality of wealth per se sits somewhat uneasily in company with state-promoted lotteries and with nature's own fortuitous dispensation of inventive genius and the singular talents of popular idols of stage and screen and sportsground. As for capacity to pay, the principle would be more rationally satisfied, not by taxing wealth per se, but by taxing the extent to which wealth is expended on the use or consumption of the community's resources— the unequal and privileged exploitation of which presently goes largely untaxed. (Society of course has reason to be concerned with socially *unacceptable* means of acquiring wealth—white collared or uncollared. And it has reason to be concerned if unequal wealth confers unequal political power. But these concerns are more appro- priately the concern of the legislature than the treasury.)

Turning finally to possible opposition on the grounds of practical- ity, discussion needs to be prefaced by keeping in mind that the prin- ciple of land value rental *already operates at the municipal level* via rates levied on the unimproved capital value of land (even though the rationale of rating on unimproved rather than improved values is not widely appreciated[3]). By capturing a small proportion of the cap- italised value of land, rates notionally capture a proportion of its annual rental value. Wider application of the concept of land value rental would require the concurrent elimination, wholly or partially, of other sources of public revenue and this, as discussed earlier, would in turn require reapportionment of inter-governmental revenue raising responsibilities, particularly in federal societies. In Australia, given an exceedingly complex tax system and a multiplicity of revenue mechanisms arbitrarily allocated between three levels of gov- ernment, disturbing their de facto equilibrium might seem a daunt- ing prospect (compounded, like many other reforms, by the shortness of parliamentary terms).

Nevertheless, the present distribution of fiscal responsibilities in Australia is such that the staged implementation of land value rental could in fact probably be initiated fairly simply.

Rates currently meet roughly about 50 percent of local government revenue needs. Most of the balance comes directly or indirectly from the Commonwealth, in effect from tax revenue. The proportions reflect assumptions about the relative capacity to pay of ratepayers and taxpayers. The proportions are essentially arbitrary and can be varied. The contribution by ratepayers could be increased, provided the burden of their contribution as taxpayers was correspondingly reduced. Thus if the Commonwealth's transfer payments to local government (raised from tax revenue) were reduced, rates levied by local government could be increased. In other words, the staged implementation of land value rental could be initiated by a reduction of income tax, financed by reducing the Commonwealth's transfer payments to local government in annual stages.

A possible alternative would be for the Commonwealth to gradually reduce its income tax reimbursement grants to the states and require the states to extend state land tax to all landholders and gradually increase its incidence (after which payroll tax, the ultimate absurdity, could be phased out[4]).

In both cases the transition could have some unforeseeable differential impacts upon particular industry sectors, or upon categories of taxpayers. These might require short-term adjustments, but over time they would be unlikely to require any fundamental dispensations or exemptions.

Transitional implementational complexities notwithstanding, a review of possible objections and likely opposition confirms the practicality of the wider adoption of land value rental beyond the limited extent to which it already operates at the municipal level. It would demonstrably resolve inequalities and incongruities that are crying out to be remedied and *for which no alternative solutions have ever been advanced. The most formidable impediment is likely to be a pervasive societal inertia: the ramifications of reform may seem too arcane and complicated and tedious to confront, and the inequities and incongruities may have become so institutionalised and long-ingrained that they are assumed to be inevitable.*

Supplementary Notes

1. An obligation to pay what has been called land value rental does *not* signify leasehold tenure or imply any diminution of "freehold ownership." Rational discussion is unfortunately fraught with terminological difficulties and inadequacies in the English language in this area. In the absence of a convenient alternative, the term "land value rental" has been used to express the notion of an annual payment in lieu of a capitalised lump sum payment. The problem, however, is that, while "rent" and "rental" derive from economic theory, in practice they are popularly associated with leasehold tenure. Their use tends to connote leasehold even though, historically, a "quit-rent" was payable in the early years of Australian colonial settlement when land was granted outright, effectively in freehold. Again, local government "rates" presently capture part of the annual rental value of land, yet the liability to pay rates does not evoke leasehold, and would not connote leasehold even if rates were equated with and captured the full annual value. *"Community charge"*—not "rent" and certainly not a "tax"—might be a more appropriate term, provided it was understood to mean an annual charge technically equal to what economics calls the annual rental value.

2. Historically this has been a somewhat sensitive issue for local authorities. While the desire of elderly people to bequeath their properties unencumbered is understandable, if they are unable to meet their rental obligations it is their beneficiary children who should contribute and not other ratepayers. In the city of Brisbane the persistence of this anachronism currently requires other ratepayers to contribute $18 million annually to make up the revenue shortfall.

3. While land, site or unimproved land value (commonly referred to as unimproved capital value or UCV)* is the accepted basis for local government rating in Queensland, New South Wales and the Australian Capital Territory, the basis for rating in some municipalities in the other states is improved land value (ICV), that is, the value of the land plus the improvements erected on it. Particularly in Victoria local referenda are held periodically to decide the rating base. That the question is open to debate may seem strange. A rate on improved value is conducive to urban blight. It penalises those who improve their properties and accordingly discourages the development of vacant land and the re-development of derelict or blighted areas. Moreover, the valuation of improved properties is generally more difficult

---

* The terms "land value," "site value" and "unimproved capital value" are synonymous for present purposes in that they all exclude improvements *on* land. Technically, however, land value and site value specifically recognise that improvements *to* land (such as filling, drainage and levelling) may have occurred over time through human intervention and become merged in what was, theoretically, the land's natural state.

than valuing land; and property owners can evade their obligations in some cases if improvements are difficult for the valuer to detect. Yet local option polls have been vigorously contested, and the Victorian government has indicated its preference for rating on improved values. Support for ICV rating stems from a curious mixture of self-interested and misconceived motivations. On the one hand, support comes from major landowners and land speculators who pay less under ICV rating if their land is unimproved. On the other hand, some poorer localities are tempted to assume that substantial improvements are an obvious indication of a capacity to pay, which should therefore be exploited. This argument is emotively plausible if expressed in terms of poor families having to pay the same land rates as their wealthy neighbours. Viewed in isolation simply as a wealth tax, ICV rating can thus attract popular support. But this muddies the waters and represents a departure from the benefit principle, which is the true rationale of local government rating— the community should be reimbursed in proportion to the extent to which property owners benefit from occupying the community's land resources and from the services provided by the community. Local option polls unfortunately reflect in microcosm the misconceptions and confusion that abound in the wider community about property valuation and the rationale of public revenue raising.

4. Although in this instance a problem would be that, while all citizens would become liable (directly or indirectly) for land tax, not all citizens would be direct beneficiaries of the abolition of payroll tax. Be this as it may, unscrambling the existing revenue raising mixture could be assisted in various ways by increasing the emphasis upon land value and upon user charges. Stamp duty, for example, is a deterrent to mobility and a regressive revenue tax except to the extent to which it is a user charge for the administration of registration.

Chapter 10

Henry George Re-Visited

THE CENTRAL MESSAGE OF THE PRECEDING CHAPTERS IS NOT NEW. It has been propounded before—more than a century ago. It was propounded in 1879 by American social philosopher and political economist Henry George, whose best known book *Progress and Poverty* was republished in millions of copies and translated into 15 languages. It had a profound influence upon socio-economic debate for some 50 years thereafter, and an impact upon land administration policy and practice in many parts of the world, not least in Australia and New Zealand at the time of federation.

The fact that this may surprise some present-day readers is part of the enigma that this present volume has sought to address. Around the turn of the century, his name was a household word. Yet today, only a relatively small band of dedicated adherents are familiar with Henry George's writing, and economics and commerce students can complete their university courses without ever having heard his name.

The original version of *Progress and Poverty* ran to nearly 600 pages. An easier reference is the 238-page centenary edition published in 1979.[1] Even so, George's somewhat florid 19th-century style (adorned with a scholarly wealth of historical, classical and biblical allusions) and his frequent recourse to homespun, albeit shrewdly perceptive, analogies tend to cloud his message for 20th-century readers. His extensive refutation of Malthus, for example, is outdated (in the terms in which it was couched), and his elaboration of marginal utility theory is unnecessary. Which is fortunate, because events since 1879 have arguably increased the relevance of basic Georgist philosophy and can be shown to have significantly increased the practicability of its implementation.

For present purposes the essential elements of Georgism can be sufficiently distilled. Henry George set out to address a paradox. For him the enigma was the paradox patently evident in Anglo-American

American Journal of Economics and Sociology, Vol. 64, No. 5 (November, 2005).
© 2005 American Journal of Economics and Sociology, Inc.

society of his time: the paradox of continuing poverty and inequality, notwithstanding the technological advances of the industrial era, which should have improved the human condition and advanced the happiness and welfare of all members of society. The pervasive theme of *Progress and Poverty* is thus quite literally expressed in its title.

The paradox of course persists, arguably in sharper focus—even if 20th-century sensibilities, resigned to its long continuance, have been inured by complacent acceptance of its seeming inevitability.

The essence of the Georgist remedy can be paraphrased quite simply: *in any community the revenue needed for community purposes should be raised by requiring all occupiers of the community's land to reimburse the community in proportion to the value of their share of the land, instead of requiring them to pay taxes levied on the income earned from their labour.* This, George argued, would go to the heart of the paradox by mitigating poverty and inequality. The obligation to pay an annual rent to the community would reduce, indeed eliminate, the price of land. Affordable access would therefore be opened up to land being withheld from productive use by speculators. The accumulation of unearned wealth from community-created land values would be thwarted. Wage and salary earners would be relieved of the burden of taxes levied on the income earned from their labour and skills. And the owners of capital would similarly be relieved of the burden of taxes levied on the interest earned from productive investment of their capital.

These are essentially the benefits that have been argued, deductively, in Chapters 6 and 7. In *Progress and Poverty* George's approach was a protracted analysis of the relationship between the three factors of production: land, labour and capital. By demonstrating that all production derives from the application of labour and capital to land, that capital is essentially wealth created by labour and that land is in finite supply while labour and capital are variables, his aim was to show how an increase in production created by the application of labour and/or capital increased the value of land. This increase in the value of land increased the proportion of wealth, which an owner of land required for production could claim, either by way of increased rent or an increased selling price. Since the supply of land was finite, an owner of land could control its market supply. Without any contribution of labour or capital himself, he stood to gain whenever an increase in population or community development required an increase in production.

Central to the Georgist argument of course is recognition of the unique character of land. As a finite resource provided by nature, land was fundamentally different from labour and capital, which represented, respectively, human effort and the accumulated means of production acquired by human effort. Thus George argued that, if land needed for a productive enterprise was held by a private owner, what was left for labour (by way of wages or salary) and what was left for capital (by way of profit or interest) would be determined by what was left after the landowner claimed his rent or sale price. In other words, the *relative shares* of labour and capital in the rewards of an enterprise, and indeed the viability of the enterprise, would depend on the availability and quality of labour (or alternative technology) and the cost of interest on capital. But the *proportion* of return that labour and capital *together* obtained from an enterprise was dependent upon the proportion taken out in land rent or land price by whoever controlled the availability of the land needed for the enterprise.

That any individual should be in a position to profit from controlling the availability of a naturally provided resource was in George's view an indefensible anachronism that frustrated productive employment and conferred unearned wealth on the possessors of land. Argued in these terms, George's proposition offered a potentially persuasive solution to the perceived shortcomings of capitalism and the paradox of poverty amidst progress.

Yet in spite of the world-wide attention that George's writing attracted and the enthusiastic endorsement of many eminent adherents, Georgism did not inspire mass political action. Fortuitously, on the critical question of the relationship between land, labour and capital, the practitioners of Marxism diverged.

Henry George was, consistently and repeatedly, an avowed exponent of a genuinely competitive free market economy in the classical tradition. For him its operation was flawed by the private appropriation of community-created land values. For Marx, on the other hand, capitalism was fatally flawed by what he saw as the inherently unequal and irreconcilable conflict between capital and labour for the rewards of productive enterprise. Choosing to overlook the fact that, historically, capital was the product of labour, Marxism in practice, notwithstanding Book 3 of *Das Kapital*, chose not to recognise that capital and labour were jointly aligned against land, and that the enemy of both was the private landowner who could manipulate the supply of a natural resource and reap unearned land value profits as a result of the productivity of capital and labour.

For the purposes of political action, Marx's disciples found the image of the plutocratic capitalist a more readily assimilable incitement to revolutionary fervour than that of the rent-seeking landowner whose role was less easily discernible (and who could in any case be loosely lumped together with capital owners under the pejorative appellation of capitalist). In the event, although its derivative tyrannies have since proved disastrous in practice, Marxism inspired mass political action. Georgism did not. One is left to speculate about the consequences for world history in the 20th century if Marx had not diverged in favour of a plausible but flawed revolutionary cause and had endorsed Georgist philosophy instead.

Another much earlier circumstance illustrates how—again fortuitously—conventional economic wisdom evolved antipathetically to Georgist philosophy in one critical respect. What may be the genesis of conditioned opposition to Georgism can be located within the monumental work of Adam Smith. The genius of Adam Smith identified the role of the "invisible hand" in the interaction of supply and demand, and established the rationale and theoretical framework for a free market economic system, which would subsequently accommodate the Industrial Revolution and survive effectively intact to the present day. A century earlier than Henry George, Smith spelt out the relationship between the factors of production and recognised the subversion of competition by monopoly landholding. He asserted that land values were "peculiarly" suitable for taxation. Land could not be hidden, land values were readily measurable at modest cost, and a tax on land caused least distortion to the operation of commerce and industry. Yet Adam Smith explicitly exempted *vacant* land (on the grounds that, while it was unused, it was not providing its owner with an income).

This fortuitous aberration is difficult to reconcile with Smith's mainstream philosophy. It seems explicable only as a conditioned reflection of the privileged self-interest assumed, as of right, by the property-owning establishment classes of his time. Notwithstanding extensions of the franchise, the predominance of property owners in government extended into the 20th century and, significantly, the influence of Smith's exemption of vacant land has survived to the present day in English (though not in Scottish) property rating practice.

One may wonder, too, about another fortuitous event. The course of socio-economic history might conceivably have been different, and the climate of 20th-century opinion might have been more favourable to Georgism, if the development of an embryonic theory of resources rental by the 18th-century French Physiocrats (whom Adam Smith admired) had not been curtailed by the advent of a revolution—a revolution that symbolically enshrined liberty and fraternity, but did little to inhibit increasing economic inequality. At pages 141–142 George cites the thwarted prospect of radically new fiscal legislation in France as "one of the things most to be regretted about the French Revolution." (Modern observers may see a parallel in the failure of Mrs. Aquino's "people power" revolution to find an alternative economic model.)

Progress and Poverty goes on to test the concept of land value rental as a source of public revenue against the accepted principles of taxation. George identifies its beneficiaries and its likely opponents. And, in a particularly important and scholarly chapter, he traces the evolution of currently accepted notions of property rights in land. He reviews the influence of Roman law upon the decline in Western societies of tribal and feudal concepts of communal ownership; and how abolition of the obligation of service to the state, which feudalism attached to the private possession of land, far from being a "triumph of freedom," conferred absolute ownership on privileged landholders and saddled the community at large with the burden of ever-increasing taxation. Thorold Rogers's *Six Centuries of Work and Wages* had not been written in 1879. George would have welcomed its affirmation that the "golden age" of the English labourer began to fade after the common lands were enclosed and the baronial elite claimed absolute ownership of the land of the realm.[2]

George's final chapters amount to an eloquent but protracted peroration, liberally laced with philosophical speculation. George projects an elegantly extravagant vision of a universally reformed society, but they add little of substance.

Re-visiting Henry George is a curious experience. His voluminous writings are a kaleidoscopic canvas, and attempting a highly abbreviated distillation is fraught with risk. A century later, however, much of the content can be discarded. Partly because it is no longer necessary to refute anachronistic theories prevalent in the 1880s (or contest the "wages fund" concept cherished by employer organisations); and marginal utility theory and even Ricardo's law of rent are not strictly relevant to George's basic argument. Partly also because his vigorous refutation of Malthus is an unnecessary digression that, like other needlessly overstated assertions, provoked a great deal of diversionary debate. Whether Malthus—seen in the context of 1879—was right is irrelevant. Malthusian theory simply provided George with a convenient opportunity to argue that food production was not limited "naturally" but by the man-caused withholding of land from productive use in order to profit from its increased value. As a debating point, a valid enough argument in 1879. And still valid today, although even if all suitable land were brought into production, and allowing for scientific discoveries that are yet to materialise, it seems barely conceivable that the planet's capacity to feed its inhabitants is not, ultimately, limited. However, the focus of Neo-Malthusian debate has changed. In relation to food production, population growth is not an accelerating crisis.[3] There is less scope for theological disputation. The focus now is more properly on environmental sustainability and, as argued earlier (in Chapter 4), on the demographic implications of structural unemployment. In respect of the latter, Georgism would increase access to land for productive use (as well as for individual subsistence), assuming there was a market for the products of labour. (But the scope for employing an increasing population would be limited if the lifestyle aspirations of society's economically dominant elite continued to be better met by capital-intensive labour-displacing technology.)

None of these Malthusian considerations, however, has any real bearing upon the validity of the basic Georgist proposition.

Again, whether or not poverty in America was increasing in 1879, as George implied, is beside the point. And the notion of land rental sufficing as a "single tax" for all public revenue needs is an unnecessary over-simplification (admittedly more commonly propagated subsequently by others than by George himself). Issues such as these were bound to generate disagreement and obfuscation, particularly since neither George nor his contemporary detractors chose to adduce statistical evidence.

Progress and Poverty provoked voluminous international and interdisciplinary reaction ranging from enthusiastic endorsement to vituperative opposition and dismissal. George was condemned variously as an agrarian socialist, as an apologist for capitalism, and as an agent of the devil. Reviewing his ideas in 1909, *Palgrave's Dictionary of Political Economy* warned: "The danger of these opinions has become more apparent as time goes on."

Much of the criticism that *Progress and Poverty* evoked can be attributed to George's variable terminology and loose use of language in different contexts in the course of a very long book and in his copious other writings. Some of the adverse reaction, however, appears to have been attributable to quite inexcusable misconceptions, prompting Tolstoy's oft-quoted assertion that "people do not argue with the teaching of George, they simply do not know it."

One of the most destructive and inaccurate misinterpretations has always been that Georgism means the confiscation and nationalisation of all land and its conversion to leasehold tenure. George had no illusions about the opposition his philosophy would generate among landowners. He was at pains to emphasise that he was not proposing the confiscation of private land. The obligation to reimburse the community annually for claiming a share of the community's land resources would not require any landowner to part with his land. It would merely make it unprofitable not to use the land and would therefore deter the speculative withholding of unused or under-used land in the hope of future land value increases (created, not by the landowner, but by population growth and community development). But the misinterpretation has been cultivated by Georgism's detractors and still prevails.

Unfortunately, George himself is partly to blame. At page 129 (of the centenary edition) he explicitly affirms the continuance of private land ownership: "I do not propose either the purchase or the confiscation of private property in land . . . Let the individuals who now hold it . . . buy and sell and bequeath and devise it. *It is not necessary to confiscate land: it is only necessary to confiscate rent."* Again, at page 130: "In form, the ownership of land would remain just as now. No owner of land need be dispossessed and no restriction need be placed upon the amount of land anyone could hold." Yet in a different context on the same and preceding pages he uses the terms "common ownership" and "common property."

The fact of course is that leasehold is a limited and conditional form of tenure for a specified term of years, whereas the Georgist proposition envisages the continuance of freehold tenure and full and exclusive ownership rights of inheritance and disposal, subject only to the payment of an annual fee—conveniently called a rent but more appropriately conceived as a community charge—to the community for public purposes (in lieu of other taxes).

Thus an understanding of Henry George's position requires an understanding that it involves the continuance of private land ownership. It requires an understanding of his definitions of land, labour and capital and their relationship. And, above all, it requires recognition of the special status of land as a finite natural resource fundamentally distinguishable from man-made goods and structures. Reduced to these prerequisites, it is difficult to equate Georgism with revolutionary heresies of the devil incarnate.[4]

What, then, is to be learned from re-visiting Henry George? Do the circumstances that influenced the climate of economic debate in the late 19th century throw any light upon the enigma that the present volume seeks to address, the enigma of why the seemingly persuasive logic of George's proposition has not been more vigorously pursued given the universal attention that his writing initially attracted? Morally and socially unsustainable though it may be, the opposition of major landowners is understandable and tangible. Other opposition is elusive. That it persists and why it persists is the larger enigma that encompasses the continuing paradox of poverty amidst progress.

Part of the answer may lie with George's dated writing style and the convolutions of presentation and sequence necessitated by his gratuitous digressions into peripheral issues. In part, however, it may be that society is awaiting a revival and updating of Georgist philosophy in 20th-century terms. *If so, there are indeed additional arguments now that were not present in 1879 and that considerably reinforce the Georgist position.*

For example, the advent of comprehensive town planning schemes, which control the uses to which land can be put and thereby have a major and direct bearing upon the value of any given parcel of land. A productive combination of labour and capital will continue to enhance the value of land, but a town planning approval granted by a community planning agency may enhance its value dramatically overnight. The inequity of allowing windfall profits to be appropriated by private landholders can thus be demonstrated more clearly than in George's day. And the status of land as a community resource, controlled and enhanced in value by the community's decisions, is arguably more apparent now than in 1879.

Secondly, the technical feasibility of annual (or more frequent) re-valuations now means that valuations for the purpose of calculating annual rental can be kept up to date and thus more accurately reflect changes (both upward and downward) in current market value in response to changes in economic circumstances.

Thirdly, while national taxation authorities in an increasingly complex society are striving to plug loopholes and minimise avoidance and evasion of conventional taxes, the scope for both legitimate avoidance and money laundering is widening through the proliferation of transnational industry and commerce and the increasing mobility of capital. For nations trying to preserve their economic identity, contemporary trends highlight the merits of a fiscal regime that is based on an *immobile* public revenue source and requires only minimal compliance costs.

At the same time, a fourth circumstance can be identified with even more fundamental global implications. The later years of the 20th century have witnessed increasing recognition and endorsement of the notion of environmentally sustainable development—across national boundaries and, significantly, among younger age groups. While the ways and means of precisely identifying environmental thresholds are uncertain, and while substantive national commitments to unilateral and/or collective action are ill-defined, there can be no doubt that any meaningful pursuit of sustainable development must come to terms with the valuation and pricing of the planetary community's natural resources and with eliminating development pressures that are primarily motivated by the prospect of windfall private profits. Otherwise, if the environmental movement remains largely dependent upon exhortation and subjective (and sometimes extravagant) assertions, its efforts will be effectively vitiated.

Thus four factors can be identified that arguably render Georgist philosophy more relevant and more persuasive today than in George's time and administratively more amenable to practical implementation.

Bearing in mind that the private appropriation of land values is an escalating source of wealth to major landowners, readers familiar with Henry George's lamentation of economic disparity, public corruption and declining faith in democratic institutions (pp. 202 et seq., centenary edition), might be disposed to add a fifth, albeit less tangible, factor: the indications in the later decades of the 20th century of increasing socio-economic inequality and a concomitant and widening subversion of morality.

Given the additional arguments that can be adduced, is it possible to envisage a resurgence of Georgist philosophy? The following chapter reviews more specifically some of the opposition that Henry George encountered and why recognition and acceptance of his philosophy has proved so elusive. And why, regrettably, the enigma of his non-acceptance may yet endure.

Supplementary Notes

1. The Hogarth Press, London, 1979.

2. "I have stated more than once that the fifteenth century and first quarter of the sixteenth were the golden age of the English labourer, if we are to interpret the wages which he earned by the cost of the necessaries of life. At no time were wages ... so high, and at no time was food so cheap. Attempts were constantly made to reduce these wages by Act of Parliament ... But these efforts were futile" J. E. Thorold Rogers, *Six Centuries of Work and Wages—The History of English Labour*, Fisher Unwin, London, 14th edition, 1919, p. 326. Curiously, for all Thorold Rogers's detailed historical

exposition of the impact on both capital and labour of the diversion of wealth into the pockets of the landowning elite, he too misconstrued Henry George and assumed that he proposed the nationalisation of land and the creation of an inflated bureaucracy to administer it. In a somewhat anti-climactic final chapter, Rogers, while endorsing the taxation of ground rent (as distinct from structural improvements), appears to have pinned his faith on the strengthening of organised labour.

Compare also Richard Cobden in the (UK) parliamentary debate on the Corn Laws in 1845: "For a period of 150 years after the Conquest, the whole of the revenue of the country was derived from the land. During the next 150 years it yielded nineteen-twentieths of the revenue. For the next century down to the reign of Richard III it was nine-tenths. During the next 70 years to the time of Mary it fell to about three-fourths. From this time to the end of the Commonwealth, land appeared to have yielded one half of the revenue. Down to the reign of Anne it was one-fourth. In the reign of George III it was one-sixth. For the first 30 years of his reign the land yielded one-seventh of the revenue. From 1793 to 1816 (during the period of the land tax), land contributed one-ninth. From which time to the present (1845) one-twenty-fifth only has been derived from the land . . . Thus, the land which anciently paid the whole of taxation paid now only a fraction . . . The people had fared better under the despotic monarchs than when the powers of the state had fallen into the hands of a landed oligarchy who had first exempted themselves from taxation, and next claimed compensation for themselves by a corn law for their heavy and peculiar burdens."

3. World population has not increased exponentially as Malthus predicted. Seemingly, social and economic development and improvements in the status and education of women have been no less effective than the draconian measures adopted in China; and food production per capita has significantly increased (albeit not uniformly). See, for example, Amartya Sen's "Population: Delusion and Reality" in the *New York Review* of 22.9.94.

4. It is interesting to compare Henry George's analysis of the creaming off of the rewards of capital and labour by landowners with the views of the then President of the UK Board of Trade, Winston Churchill, some 30 years later: "It is quite true that land monopoly is not the only monopoly which exists, but it is by far the greatest of monopolies—it is a perpetual monopoly, and it is the mother of all other forms of monopoly" (*The People's Rights*, Jonathan Cape, London, 1970, p. 117; first published in 1909). And: "It does not matter where you look or what examples you select, you will see that every form of enterprise, every step in material progress, is only undertaken after the land monopolist has skimmed the cream off for himself, and everywhere today the man or public body who works to put land to its highest use is forced to pay a preliminary fine in land values to the man who is putting it to an inferior use, and in some cases to no use at all. All comes

back to the land value, and its owner for the time being is able to levy his toll upon all other forms of wealth and upon every form of industry" (p. 121). Churchill's views remained consistent. It was during his wartime prime ministership that the three great commissions of inquiry were appointed in anticipation of post-war reconstruction, most pertinently for present purposes the Uthwatt Commission on Compensation and Betterment.

Chapter 11

Apathy, Cupidity or Conspiracy?

THE PARADOX OF the co-existence of progress and poverty was the enigma that Henry George addressed. He propounded a seemingly logical and persuasive means of mitigating the paradox. A century later, extremes of wealth and poverty still co-exist. They have not been substantially mitigated by any alternative solutions. George's remedy attracted wide-ranging support in his time and has since been endorsed in principle by eminent people in many nations and across the political spectrum. The enigma now is why George's arguments have not prevailed.

Like re-visiting Henry George, exploring the enigma is a curiously unsatisfying experience. The trail is confused and tortuous. There must surely be an explanation. One expects to find evidence around the next corner. Yet it never quite materialises.

For the period from 1879 to 1979, the task of reviewing the opposition to George is made easier by Robert Andelson's *Critics of Henry George*, sub-titled *A Centenary Appraisal of Their Strictures on Progress and Poverty*.[1] In the course of 26 chapters Andelson and an international panel of contributors review the major critics of *Progress and Poverty*, grouped as "Nineteenth Century British and Continental Critics, Nineteenth Century American Critics, and Twentieth Century Critics." These reviews of major critics are prefaced by a scholarly introductory chapter in which Andelson summarises the views of a very wide range of other critics whose criticisms he did not select for examination in detail. Their views were either already substantially covered by those selected, or were primarily directed ad hominem— for example, by the then newly emerging economics discipline at George the self-educated political economist and social philosopher (who in turn amply reciprocated the hostility).

As an economist, George was indeed self-taught, as of course were

American Journal of Economics and Sociology, Vol. 64, No. 5 (November, 2005).
© 2005 American Journal of Economics and Sociology, Inc.

all his predecessors extending back to Adam Smith. His status, however, cannot seriously be questioned. Half a century later, for example, the verdict of Joseph Schumpeter was that "he was a very orthodox economist and extremely conservative as to methods" in the English classical tradition.[2]

If they have the patience, readers may care to read Andelson and satisfy themselves about George's critics. The experience is depressing, and evokes decidedly unflattering impressions of the quality of academic debate. Very little of the criticism centres on the basic Georgist proposition. Instead, a very great deal is based on misconceptions, or is directed at peripheral issues that are not relevant to any present-day assessment of its validity and practicality.

Some misconceptions can be attributed to George's style, his inconsistent terminology and the sheer volume of his writing. For example, the misconception that he proposed the nationalisation of all land and its conversion to leasehold, referred to in the previous chapter. On the other hand, it does not require a close reading of *Progress and Poverty* to establish that George certainly did *not* propose that all men were equal and were entitled to equal shares of land (as assumed, for example, by T. H. Huxley). Nor did he propose that poverty should be remedied by an equal distribution of the aggregate national land rental revenue to all citizens. And it seems tendentious in the extreme to draw any particular conclusions from George's choice of agricultural land and labour as the most convenient exemplar of the relationship between wages and rent.

Provoked by some of George's gratuitous but incidental declarations and by exaggerations such as his implicit assumption that land monopolisation was the *only* cause of poverty, some of his critics erected diversionary straw men and expansively demolished them. Some have already been referred to. The Malthusian controversy, for example, and whether or not the conditions of labour in the 1880s were actually improving, and whether or not landowners' proportionate share of the proceeds of production had declined over time are irrelevant to any assessment of George's basic proposition. Irrelevant or not, it would seem that many such debates served as pegs upon which to hang instinctive hostility to a perceived challenge to the traditionally enshrined acceptance of landed wealth. Some critics indeed explicitly defended such a "natural" order of society, among them senior members of the Roman Catholic Church. Andelson cites Father Victor Cathrein, a Swiss-born Jesuit theologian, as "perhaps the most influential Continental European critic of Henry George." Cathrein's defence of private land ownership was subsequently echoed in Pope Leo XIII's encyclical *Rerum Novarum*, to which George responded in an open letter (in 1881). But these exchanges are sterile and irrelevant today. Denial and denigration of the tribal concept of communal ownership belong to theology rather than history. Ironically, it can be argued that Leo XIII's denunciation of Henry George in *Rerum Novarum* contributed to the spread of Marxism as seemingly the only alternative to laissez-faire capitalism.

Some concerns, however, were expressed by more credible critics and remain topical. Thus in the light of the increasing demands upon government in modern society, George's assumption that land value rental, the "single tax," would raise sufficient public revenue for all the needs of government has been questioned (by Schumpeter among others). But this does not in itself detract from the merits of taxing land instead of labour and capital.

It has also been contended that, at least in some circumstances, some *part* of increased land value can be attributed to the quality of development constructed by individual landholders rather than being *wholly* attributable to public planning decisions or to population growth and general community development.[3]

Another objection, or more accurately an expression of puzzlement (which still prevails), stems from misconceiving the effect on a parcel of land of claiming its full annual rental for the community and assuming that its value would thereby be reduced to zero. The explanation of course is that, while its *value* remains the same, its selling *price* (capitalised rental value) would indeed be reduced to zero (since its owner would no longer be able to capitalise its rental value). Again, both before and since Andelson's review, some critics have contended that the amount of speculation in land is not sufficiently important to warrant endeavouring to suppress it. But this can hardly be sustained in the light of the statistical evidence (in Chapter 3), or in the light of the emasculation and distortion of the planning system by speculatively inspired development proposals.

Surprisingly, some modern critics of land speculation have nevertheless misunderstood Henry George.[4] On the other hand, a number of current economics texts explicitly endorse the taxation of land,[5] and it is a little surprising therefore that the Association for Land Value Taxation was denied attendance at the then Prime Minister's much-publicised and purportedly widely representative "National Tax Summit" in Australia in 1985.

By far the most important and potentially controversial question not adequately dealt with in *Progress and Poverty* relates to timing. The introduction of a land value rental regime would not involve the confiscation of land or the disturbance of existing ownership. It would, however, effectively involve confiscation of future rental profits. Andelson therefore discusses spreading the introduction of land value rental gradually over a period of years.[6]

The question of timing and other questions of substance and implementation have been addressed in detail in earlier chapters. In the present chapter they have been alluded to briefly in the course of the quest for clues that may explain why, historically, the Georgist concept of land value rental has failed to gain acceptance. In the event, however, it seems that one must look further than any specific objections. Partly because none are conclusive. Partly also because, paradoxically, a number of George's critics conceded a measure of sympathy with his objectives and even, in the course of their convoluted and ambivalent responses, qualified their opposition and tried to accompany George along part of the way.

That Georgism, after its initial impact, failed to materialise as a mass movement while Marxism, in spite of its internal contradictions and ambiguities, succeeded has been the subject of debate. Even though George was nearly successful in contesting the New York mayoralty (in 1886), it seems the Georgist movement tended to eschew organised political action. Georgist philosophy required intellectual debate. Whereas Marxism lent itself to being channelled with revolutionary fervour into a simple emotive crusade against undifferentiated inequalities in wealth, and could be readily manipulated by power-seeking demagogues and political activists, Georgism required distinguishing between forms of wealth and an understanding of the economic implications of private ownership of one special kind of wealth. As an economic doctrine Marxism has been tried and discredited. Georgism has not been tried. Part of the explanation may be in its failure to generate political action.

Leaving aside the considerable capacity for conceptualising required to fully appreciate the logic of the Georgist position, another clue may be that, paradoxically, the essential Georgist proposition, that is, "taxing" land instead of labour, seems *too simple* to be believable. Disbelief and scepticism are not allayed by George's flamboyant prose and his images of a "Golden Age" and "the culmination of Christianity—the City of God on earth." Nor are they allayed by the less flamboyant but equally extravagant claims of some of his latter-day adherents whose proselytising endeavours tend to portray land value rental as a snake-oil-type panacea for all society's ills.

Be this as it may, no amount of surmising is wholly satisfying. Progress and poverty continue to co-exist, subsumed within the large enigma. The fact remains that a land value rental system *could* provide the bulk of public revenue without recourse to taxes that penalise productive labour and enterprise. It *could* be an alternative to arbitrary taxing mechanisms that entail enormous public and private compliance costs, yet can readily be evaded by the ingenious, the powerful and the dishonest. It *could* eliminate inflationary private profiteering in land, preserve the integrity of the planning system and guarantee the availability of funds for community infrastructure and services. It *could* deter the unproductive diversion of investment capital into property and safeguard the environment from urban sprawl and speculative development. It *could* ensure that possession of land did not exacerbate social and economic inequality. It *could* ensure affordable access to land for housing and, while it would not of itself eliminate the displacement of labour by technology, it *could* similarly ensure more affordable access to land for all who wished to undertake productive activities. And, while unanimity on most economic issues is almost infinitely elusive, virtually all economists are agreed that charges on the unimproved value of land are the least distorting of all the means of public revenue raising. If these are all desirable, indeed urgent, societal objectives, nothing suggests that they will be or can be achieved by any other means.[7]

In the pursuit of reform the former communist countries face transitional problems including practical difficulties associated with inadequate land title registration facilities and rudimentary land planning and valuation systems. Western societies have no such practical problems. They have well-established titles registries, adequate cadastral maps and increasingly sophisticated land use planning systems that determine the use to which any given parcel of land can be put, and thus its value, subject to market demand. And while in the past the infrequency of periodic valuations made it difficult to raise revenue equitably and efficiently by way of rates or charges on land, this is no longer the case. In other words, in the Western world *there are no technical or administrative obstacles in the way of raising public revenue by charges upon land.* And in much of the Western world *local* government already does so.

Nevertheless, one conceivable clue to the enigma may lie in inadequate public understanding of the workings of government in this area. As a separate professional discipline, town planning has emerged only in comparatively recent times. Its status and that of town plans has been uncertain, and the potentially decisive influence of planning upon land value has not been fully appreciated. It is also true that land valuation has not been accorded the same status as disciplines such as economics and the other social sciences. While suspected monopolistic tendencies in the land market have long been a source of concern and resentment, the significance of the relationship between public authority decisions and land values has not always been sufficiently appreciated.

The fact that some local authorities persist in levying rates on *improved* property values, notwithstanding that it penalises desirable improvements, is a source of confusion.[8] So also is the successful propagation by the development industry of its need for an "incentive," and the equally spurious notion that any charges levied on land will be passed on to the industry's end consumers (notably the low income "battlers" beloved by the tabloid press).

In any democratic society, of course, the status quo, reinforced by bureaucratic inertia, is likely to prevail unless enough people understand and support the need for change. Change is even more likely to be slow if democracy is interpreted to mean that all decisions must be decisions that a popular majority endorses. This makes change particularly difficult when, for example, taxation law and policy have become so complex that it is almost impossible to achieve an informed popular consensus about reform.

At best, however, all the foregoing conjecture affords only a partial explanation. *At the heart of the matter is the nature and status of land.* The one fundamental obstacle to reform in Western societies is a mindset that has persisted for centuries and become so institutionalised that anything different is almost unthinkable. It is the mindset nurtured and sustained by the assumption that, *unlike air and water* (and unlike minerals *under* the land and forests *on* the land), raw land is a natural resource that can nevertheless be treated like man-made commodities and privately appropriated and exploited for private profit.[9] For those who can afford it, private ownership of land is an ambition. While the profits perceived to be made by big landholders are deplored, all citizens *hope* to profit from owning land. Landholding is perceived to confer personal status and be a source of further wealth—even though land ownership is never absolute because town planning controls now limit the use to which private land can be put and governments have always claimed the right to acquire private land compulsorily if it is needed for public purposes (subject to the payment of compensation—including, as has been noted earlier, compensation for land values created by public planning decisions and the public provision of community infrastructure).

Whereas the notion of private ownership of parcels of air and water is inconceivably repugnant, for centuries private ownership of raw land has been taken for granted. *If the morality of this is defensible, then the inescapable inference must be that it is only the physical difficulty of subdividing air and water that has, as yet, prevented their private appropriation as well.* After discounting all the other evidence, is this then the ultimate explanation? Is it the ultimate source of the enigma? *An institutionalised mindset, hallowed by time, buttressed by vested interests whose established wealth it preserves, and reinforced at lesser levels by universal cupidity?* A mindset that brooks no attempts to convert it. Are there indeed indications, as alleged in some quarters, of a conspiracy to defend the mindset at all costs and denigrate any who dare to challenge it? Is the mindset irreversible? Is the attitude to land on which it rests impervious to moral indictment? Undoubtedly it is formidably entrenched.

Yet can society really afford to ignore the logic and morality of requiring every member of the community to contribute to public revenue in proportion to their claims upon society's resources? Given the indications of widespread disillusionment with the present reality of both capitalism and socialism—and the obvious causal links between inequality and alienation and violence—the adoption of land value rental as the most equitable and incorruptible source of public revenue would seem to be an idea whose time now is nigh. Unless the enigma is to endure, *the onus would seem to be on the defenders of a demonstrably flawed socio-economic regime to prove conclusively that it can never be otherwise.*

Supplementary Notes

1. Robert V. Andelson, ed., Associated University Presses, New Jersey and London, 1979. [In 2003–2004, Andelson revised and enlarged this work and it was published as a two-volume set. See Robert V. Andelson, ed., 2003–2004, *Critics of Henry George*, 2 vols. Malden, MA: Blackwell Publishing.]

2. *History of Economic Analysis*, Oxford University Press, 1954.

3. For example, in the case of a developer who owns sub-divided land in an area zoned for residential use, he would pay an annual rental per lot assessed on the basis of the land's value for residential purposes (and its natural attributes). If he were to erect better than average quality dwellings on some of the lots, his development would tend to increase the attractiveness of the remaining vacant lots; and it would also tend to increase the value of the land component of the erected dwellings. In both cases the annual rental value would be assessed accordingly. Clearly, in circumstances such as these a developer's development *on* the land has increased its value. It is prima facie difficult to reconcile this with the Georgist contention that all increases in land value are created by the community (by virtue of its land use planning decisions and provision of urban works and services). What it amounts to is that the rationale of land value rental needs to be expressed rather more broadly. It is the *existence of a community and its organised social structure* as well as its exercise of land use planning powers that provides a developer with the opportunity to develop and to choose the quality

of development that is likely to prove most profitable. (The developer, it should be noted, suffers no penalty unless he does not develop the remaining lots and withholds them from the market.)

4. Thus Leonie Sandercock, one time head of an urban studies school and author of *Cities for Sale* and *The Land Racket*, thought George proposed taxing land "at different rates according to the different uses to which it was being put" and dismissed Georgist theory as "much too neat" and utopian (*The Land Racket*, Australian Association of Socialist Studies, 1979, p. 79). Various other modern critics are cited by Harrison in *The Power in the Land*, Universal Books, New York, 1983, ch. 16. An example of tabloid journalism is Heilbroner's multi-edition *The Worldly Philosophers* (Simon and Schuster, New York), in which the author regales his readers with unsourced anecdotal trivia about the personal characteristics of his various economic philosopher subjects coupled with a selective smattering of their philosophies.

5. For example: "Many of the personal and family fortunes which have been made during the transition of countries such as Australia, the United States, Canada and New Zealand from places untouched by Western civilisation to nations with modern economic and social systems, have been due to the ownership of land. As the demand for land for various purposes grew, its rental value increased enormously. This has happened both to agricultural and grazing land and even more spectacularly to town and city land. As the rental payments increased, many people began to question the right of the lucky landowners to receive such 'unearned increments'. The American Henry George (1839–1897), author of a famous book called *Progress and Poverty*, was one of these. He founded a political movement . . . known as the 'single-tax movement' . . . This is not the place to attempt any assessment of the merits or demerits of George's political creed, but one important principle of distribution and taxation can be illustrated by his doctrine: Pure rent is in the nature of a 'surplus' which can be taxed *without affecting production incentives . . . a tax on rent will lead to no distortions or economic inefficiencies."* (Samuelson, Nordhaus, Richardson, Scott and Wallace, *Economics* (Vol. 1), 1992, McGraw-Hill, Sydney).

And: "There is a renewed interest in land taxation on the part of urban economists, city planners and public officials. Many of them contend that a strong case can be made on grounds of both equity and efficiency for a heavy tax on land values . . . Unlike most other taxes a tax on land does not contribute to the misallocation of resources . . . Sales and excise taxes have the effect of increasing prices and reducing output . . . In a competitive market, the imposition of an income tax . . . (has) the effect of reducing the supply of labour . . . (and causes) workers to offer less productive effort and take more leisure. In comparison, the complete inelasticity of the supply of land means that a tax on land rent has no effect on price or output and therefore does not alter resource allocation" (Jackson and McConnell, *Economics,* McGraw-Hill, Sydney, 1985, pp. 540–541).

6. Op.cit., ch. 24.

7. The private housing market can never produce housing that will be affordable by the poorest members of society. While land value rental would eliminate land price and therefore make land for housing relatively more accessible to low income earners, it would not of itself ensure the survival of a socio-economic mix in inner urban areas where land values will inevitably rise with population growth. Indeed, land value rental pre-supposes that land in inner urban areas will be assessed for annual rental purposes in strict conformity with market estimates of its attributes, including location. In every society it will be necessary for public authorities to either provide or subsidise housing to enable the poorest members of the community to be adequately housed, particularly if, as a matter of social policy, it is desired to enable a proportion of low income people to live in inner urban areas close to community facilities.

8. See note 2, Chapter 9.

9. While the same logic is not applied to land itself, in most Western societies minerals under the land and timber on the land are deemed to belong to the community and a resource rental or royalty is payable for their extraction.

Chapter 12

The Enduring Enigma

SO MUCH FOR THE ENIGMA.

In practical terms, where does pursuit of the enigma lead us? In the preceding chapters the argument has been derived from and illustrated by a necessarily detailed overview of the particular circumstances prevailing in Australia. Otherwise, argument in the abstract would have lacked substance and conviction. But, although in some particulars the Australian circumstances may not be replicated elsewhere, in essence the conclusions that can be drawn are universally applicable. Some are incontrovertible:

> Over the years land has become the source of enormous unearned wealth. Socially, economically and environmentally the consequences are demonstrably inhibiting the well-being of contemporary society. And the situation is remediable.

The likelihood and practicality of remedial action, however, is a different question. The case for rejecting a centuries-old mindset is seemingly overwhelming. Yet, however carefully and precisely the case is argued, history suggests that those with a vested interest in the status quo will contest reform with deliberate misinterpretation, obfuscation and insidiously cultivated fear and uncertainty. Assimilating the need for change may take time.

In Australia it would require substantial bi-partisan endorsement. And a commitment once made would need to be irreversible, no matter how gradual its implementation. Nevertheless, as a more mature and confident Australia approaches the new millennium, acceptance of the need to review century-old constitutional arrangements is gaining momentum. Pointers heralding the emergence of a post-materialist society suggest that it may also be an opportune time to contemplate wide-ranging cultural change. Indeed, as the shack-

American Journal of Economics and Sociology, Vol. 64, No. 5 (November, 2005).
© 2005 American Journal of Economics and Sociology, Inc.

les of out-dated constitutional arrangements forged by negotiation and compromise in a colonial context are discarded, paradoxically *one of the more enduring pre-federation ideals could, just conceivably, be revived.* The high hopes of abolishing land speculation, ardently espoused by leading advocates of federation like O'Malley, Griffith and Deakin, could eventually be realised.

There are of course issues that need to be further explored and addressed, depending upon national circumstances. Timing the extension of land value rental, for example. In societies with no tradition of absolute private land ownership, capturing the full annual rental could be contemplated in a single stage. In Western societies, however, capturing the full annual rental value, and thereby eliminating land price, would need to be implemented in stages. Nevertheless, given the political will, the transitional problems would be neither novel nor unduly daunting.

It is the longer term implications of land value capture for living standards, the structure of society and, ultimately, planetary survival that invite further research.

One aspect has been alluded to earlier but not pursued at length. Namely, the extent to which increased reliance on resources would induce a healthier recognition of the relationship between community resources and living standard and lifestyle expectations. In other words, a clearer recognition of the inflationary penalties of resorting to capital indebtedness to finance "growth" at a rate in excess of that which the community's basic resources are able to sustain. The Australian government has recently foreshadowed expanding citizenship education with a view to increasing public understanding of the functions and institutions of government. Efforts in this direction could with advantage embrace the principles and practice of public revenue raising and the implications of fiscal and monetary policy options.

Ultimately, however, the most urgent research that Western societies should be undertaking is into the implications of inequality. Intuitively, the mounting incidence of alienation, violence, lawlessness and drug dependency now bedevilling the Western world is primarily attributable not to genetic aberrations or parental inadequacies or to other contributory causes that have been with the human species from time immemorial. Or even to poverty. But to resentment of increasing *inequality* and powerlessness.

Compounded by daily media blandishments of the material rewards of greed and self-interest, inequality is manifest in obscene and growing disparities of income, the scope available to those "within the system" to profit from fraud and evasion, and, above all, the ultimate soul-destroying inequality: rejection from participation in constructive labour and relegation to perceived worthlessness. Resentment and frustration will increasingly provoke society's outcasts to exact revenge upon a society that, against all the evidence, subscribes to the comfortable illusion that its inequities will somehow be remedied by further consumption of the planet's finite resources and the mindless pursuit of further growth and labour-displacing "development."

Further development of these issues could provide overwhelming confirmation of the need for cultural change. In the meantime, it can be shown that there are no insurmountable technical impediments in the way of *gradually increasing land value charges*. Charges upon land involve no distortion of the economy or misallocation of resources. They would disadvantage only those seeking unearned wealth at the expense of the community. Nevertheless, proponents of remedial action may need to eschew extravagant claims and accept as a realistic and achievable objective the *staged* implementation of full land value rental. And over-enthusiastic disciples of Henry George will not advance their cause by simplistic advocacy of a "single tax."

Postscript

THE ENIGMA PERSISTS. The central issues remain, but the turn of the century has seen some changes of emphasis in Australia and the emergence of new contextual elements, one of which invites a brief review of the evolution of Australian land law and administration.

Thus in mid-2000 Australia adopted "a new tax system." In lieu of a wholesale goods tax (which in practice did not impact very directly on many taxpayers), a goods and services tax was introduced, purportedly in recognition of the significance of services in post-industrial society and the perceived desirability of proportionately reducing the personal income tax component of national public revenue. Once a mere 126 pages, the legislation, which enshrines a "simplified" tax system, now encompasses more than 9,000 pages, and the compliance costs, particularly for individual taxpayers and small businesses, have remained a simmering source of frustration and resentment. Assertions that the "black" economy has survived and prospered have not been convincingly refuted. Consumption of land and natural resources remains substantially untaxed. The GST is a stark reaffirmation of the pre-existing paradox: Australians who produce socially desirable goods and services are taxed for contributing *to* the community, whereas those who take *from* the community's resources are not.

The turn of the century has also seen increased concern with ecological sustainability. Ecologically sustainable development has become the explicit objective of planning legislation, focussing attention generally upon conservation and the more sustainable use of natural resources. A particular focus has been upon the inter-related issues of inland water consumption, salination, tree clearing and compliance with the Kyoto Protocol.

Efforts to restrict tree clearing have raised questions, as yet undecided, about the rights and liabilities of pastoral and agricultural landholders, particularly those who purchased or leased their properties in the previously legitimate expectation of being able to clear them of vegetation impeding their intended use. Similarly in urban areas landholders have anticipated clearing land for residential and other urban uses. A central question is whether the state, in its efforts to

reduce greenhouse gas emissions in keeping with the Kyoto Protocol, can, in the over-riding public interest, exercise its power of
eminent domain without incurring liability for compensation (except
in circumstances amounting to expropriation).

One line of argument is that, if permission to clear vegetation is
given, a benefit or betterment is conferred on landholders that ought
to be recouped by the state—certainly before any entitlement to compensation is contemplated when clearing is restricted. In other words,
the situation revives the betterment/compensation dichotomy recognised in town planning theory.

No clear policy stance has yet been adopted. However, some scope
is seen for building in incentives through the land valuation system.
If uncleared land is valued less than cleared land (for rating or taxing
purposes), there is some incentive to preserve vegetation. A problem
of course is that local government rates, at a few cents per dollar
of land value, are only a trivial proportion of Australian public
revenue. Thus the incentive effect of differential valuations will
seldom be significant. It would of course be significant if a greater
proportion of public revenue were raised from charges on land. The
possibility of this, however, is fettered by the prevailing—and quite
arbitrary—apportionment of revenue raising responsibilities between
central, state and local governments within the Australian federal
system.

At the turn of the century one can probably point to increasing
emphasis upon land management. Within the state planning systems
it has long been recognised of course that the unearned increment
in land value attributable to planning approval of more intensive use
is an incongruous anomaly that ought to be offset by systematically
requiring contributions to community infrastructure from the private
beneficiaries. As yet, however, there has been little appreciation of
the scope for an integrated philosophy of land management and
public revenue raising.

So much for shifting emphases. By far the most significant feature
of the past decade, however, has been the emergence of a new and
very different issue. In the closing years of the 20th century land
became the focus of emotionally charged public policy the ramifications and policy implications of which are slowly and tentatively

emerging. Two landmark decisions of the Australian High Court focused attention on Aboriginal "land rights" contemporaneously with a long overdue awakening of the nation's conscience, which has given rise to protracted debate about the "reconciliation process."[1]

In *Mabo*, launched by Murray Islander Eddie Mabo (*Mabo and Others v. Queensland (No. 2)* (1992), 175 CLR), the High Court demolished the fiction of *terra nullius*, the long-standing assumption that the Australian continent was vacant and unowned prior to European settlement. In *Wik* in 1996 (*Wik Peoples v. Queensland; Thayorre People v. Queensland* (1996), 141 ALR, p. 129), the High Court held that Aboriginal ownership could co-exist with pastoral leases. The (Commonwealth) Native Title Act 1993 as amended and related legislation in the states provides a means by which Aboriginal claims (to land not alienated by freehold) can be lodged and determined (variously in federal and state courts and tribunals). Hundreds of claims have been lodged, but few as yet determined, none in respect of urban land.[2]

In effect *Mabo* established that sovereignty passed to the British Crown when Captain James Cook raised the union flag on the eastern coast of the continent in 1770, but that ownership of land was not necessarily extinguished. An inherent complication of course has been that ownership as understood by Aboriginal Australians has always been conceived as communal rather than individual. Title, where it has been claimed, has therefore been in the name of tribal groups of "traditional owners." Protracted litigation is slowly proceeding in respect of unresolved claims and entitlements, and is frustrating the granting of mining tenements as well as generating uncertainty among pastoralists. The critical question is the extent to which native title has been extinguished by prior acts of exclusive possession. Effectively since *Mabo* Australia has two land tenure systems, but, notwithstanding the 1975 Racial Discrimination Act, Anglo-Australian law is inevitably dominating indigenous law and custom. Not so much because of the formal terms of the legislation but, as one indigenous activist put it, more because of "the weight behind the hammer."[3]

The Aboriginal land rights movement implies a departure from (unstated) assumptions about gradual assimilation, and it certainly represents a rejection of the paternalism that notoriously characterised Aboriginal "protection," particularly in Queensland and Western Australia, well into the 20th century. Obviously, if land were recognised as a community resource, it would do much to bridge the cultural divide and ease the reconciliation process. As yet, however, the land rights debate *owes nothing to Georgist philosophy*. Rather, it has been conducted within the orthodoxy of Australian land law, the basic principles and institutions of which were inherited when the first (convict) settlement was established, somewhat precariously, in Sydney Cove in January 1788. To this extent, if the reconciliation process means reconciling the Aboriginal concept of land with the treatment of land as a private commodity, then it is an attempt to reconcile the irreconcilable. Grants of native "title" can only narrow but not bridge the gap. Title to commodified land? In Aboriginal culture the nation is an oxymoron.

While Australian land law remains conceptually and institutionally within the common law fold, it nevertheless exhibits some distinctive characteristics, and briefly reviewing its evolution and taking stock at the beginning of the new millennium may be timely. It may help to put the land rights movement in perspective, and perhaps it may throw some light on the enigma that has been the central theme of the preceding chapters.

High principled policy directives—reflecting considerable credit on the Imperial government six months away in Whitehall[4]—were implemented with difficulty by the early colonial governors of the territory of New South Wales. It was a turbulent raw society pre-occupied initially with sustaining itself, and then with extending the frontiers of settlement in the face of a demanding natural environment and a sometimes hostile but territorially dispersed and loosely organised indigenous population, relations with whom were ambivalent.[5]

For a detailed account of land settlement in Australian (as distinct from the evolution of land law), reference should be made to Sir Stephen Roberts's definitive *History of Australian Land Settlement*.[6] Roberts discusses the attempts to reconcile the relative claims to land, initially by the military establishment and subsequently by emancipated convicts and, finally and increasingly, by free settlers.

Governor Macquarie (1809–1821) sought, for example, to regularise an ad hoc system of land grants by forbidding resale until five years had elapsed, and by instituting a system of quit-rents attaching to land grants. Land sales began to supersede grants in the time of Governor Darling, two-thirds of whose instructions from the Colonial Office related to land matters. Protracted and intense controversy was provoked by the phenomenon of "squatting," the issues being the use by pastoralist squatters of huge areas of Crown land at very low rentals, coupled with their demands for greater security of tenure, compensation for improvements and a pre-emptive right to buy the homestead portion of their "runs." Land policy was the subject of vituperous exchanges between W. C. Wentworth and Governor Gipps (1838–1846), who frustrated Wentworth's bizarre attempt to buy from Maori chiefs some 20 million acres of New Zealand (then a dependency of New South Wales) at the rate of 100 acres per farthing. It is interesting to note (in the course of the controversy over the fees imposed on squatters) Gipps's retort that "to take a rent for the use of Crown land is not to impose a tax."

While regularising the phenomenon of squatting dominated land policy debate, the middle decades of the 19th century also saw a vast increase in population following the gold discoveries, and increasing demands for representative government. By the turn of the century, New South Wales and its then divested sister colonies of Victoria and Queensland had developed sophisticated and innovative systems of land administration and registration encompassing both freehold and Crown leasehold tenure. A respected land economist and legal historian, Judge Rae Else-Mitchell, in a tribute to the 19th-century land reformers, has said that their practical achievements "far exceeded anything which had been accomplished in the United States of America or the United Kingdom."[7]

Land scandals, particularly in Victoria in the 1880s, generated a widespread resolve (reinforced by Henry George's visit to Australia in 1890) to eliminate land speculation—culminating in the adoption, following federation in 1901, of leasehold tenure for the territory for the seat of federal government (the 900-square-mile Australian Capital Territory in which Canberra is located).

One can only speculate about the subsequent evolution of land law and administration if a remarkable bill introduced by Samuel

Griffith, premier of Queensland, in 1890 had become law. Seeking to ensure a "proper distribution of the products of labour," the bill for an Act to be cited as the Elementary Property Law of Queensland "to declare the Natural Law relating to the Acquisition and Ownership of Private Property" enunciated "First Principles," among them that "[t]he right to take advantage of natural forces belongs equally to all the members of the community"; that "[l]and, by natural law, is the common property of the community"; and that "[a]ll property, other than land, is the product or result of labour."

Alas, in what must rank as one of the significant accidents of political and social history, because of political instability and the looming economic crisis of the early 1890s, the bill lapsed (and Griffith became chief justice of Queensland and went on to become the first chief justice of the High Court of Australia).

Summing up, in what must necessarily be a highly fragmented overview, Australian land administration is characterised by some curious paradoxes. Georgist philosophy is today virtually unknown and unacknowledged. Yet, at the local government level, land value taxation has been practised for more than a century. The state land valuation authorities in Queensland and New South Wales, for example, annually assess the unimproved value of all land for state and local government purposes as a matter of course.[8] Australian valuers would be surprised at the extent to which American valuers appear to regard this as problematic and more difficult than valuing improved property. It is similarly bemusing to Australians to realise that the cause of land value taxation is frustrated in England and Scotland by the failure of the legatee of the Domesday Book to maintain a land valuation system over the centuries since 1086.

On the debit side of any scorecard of course, the trivial proportion of total national public revenue raised by local government rates has frustrated research into the impact of land value charges upon, for example, curbing urban sprawl and inducing the more productive use of vacant or underutilised land.[9] The limited scope for encouraging the preservation of natural vegetation via differential land valuation has been alluded to earlier.

Perhaps more particularly for U.S. readers it may be worth mentioning a factor that bears upon the rationale of land value taxation and capturing the betterment arising from public land use decisions, namely, the significance of the latter in establishing land values. Whether land use decisions are called town planning decisions or simply land management decisions, they are a critical determinant of land value in Australia and the United Kingdom where there is bipartisan acceptance of land use management, by whatever name, as a necessary function of government (and not a "socialist" option). Arguably the prime, indeed ultimate, determinant of land value in modern society is its permitted or permissible use. Some Georgist writers seem reluctant to recognise this. Yet it is surely the most clearcut exemplification of the Georgist contention that, whatever its natural attributes, *the market value of land for valuation purposes* is established by *public* land use decisions and an infrastructural environment created or authorised by *public* instrumentalities.

*   *   *   *   *

Reviewing the evolution of land law and administration in pursuit of the enigma, one is confronted with inter-related practical and theoretical issues (and misconceptions), the multiplicity of which may in part explain societal and governmental inertia about land reform. The logic of capturing the rental value of land (and other natural resources) for the community is indisputable. Yet the requisite commitment by the Western world is frustrated by the seeming complexity of the issues and by the vested interests that are perceived to stand in the way.

Arguably, however, the real obstacle is the long-ingrained and culturally institutionalised *acceptance* of inequities and incongruities, which date a long way back in time to a common origin. And in this the history of land law is instructive. The common origin is, demonstrably, the fateful commodification of land in the Middle Ages (and, by inference, the commodification of other natural resources). Over the ensuing centuries commodification and the privatisation of the unearned increment have enshrined private profit-seeking. Dollar darwinism has been applauded and endorsed by neo-liberal economic ideology and corporate globalisation.

Vested private interests in land and property, however, are merely a symptom of socio-economic malaise, not the main obstacle to reform. Eventually, just conceivably, a change may come if the common origin is more clearly perceived—the common origin of increasing inequality, intractable unemployment, corporate scandals and endemic greed and self-interest, the profligate pursuit of "development," the pervasive alienation and insecurity and the erosion of communitarian values and institutions.

The commodification of land and other resources may be impossible to reverse. But what most certainly can be done to minimise the inequities and incongruities is to capture the insidiously ubiquitous *unearned increment* in commodified land values.

Supplementary Notes

1. Aborigines were not recognised by the Australian Constitution or entitled to vote in elections until a constitutional referendum carried (overwhelmingly) in 1967.

2. The vast bulk of the Australian continent is non-urban land comprising Crown land or land held under various forms of Crown leasehold.

3. Wensing E. & Sheehan J., 2002, "Planners and native title" in *Australian Planner*, PIA, Vol. 39:3.

4. The Admiralty's 1768 instructions to James Cook included the following injunction: "You are likewise to observe the genius, temper, disposition and number of the natives, if there be any, and endeavour by all proper means to cultivate a friendship and alliance with them showing them every kind of civility and regard. You are also with the consent of the natives to take possession of convenient situations in the country in the name of the King of Great Britain, or, if you find the country uninhabited take possession for His Majesty by setting up proper marks and inscriptions as first discoverers and possessors."

Secretary of State Earl Grey's 1848 instruction is particularly interesting in the light of the *Wik* decision: "I think it essential that it should be generally understood that leases granted for this [pastoral] purpose give the grantees only an exclusive right of pasturage for their cattle, and of cultivating such land as they may require within the large limits thus assigned to them, but that these leases are not intended to deprive the natives of their former right to hunt over these districts or to wander over them in search of subsistence, in the manner to which they have been heretofore accustomed, from the spontaneous produce of the soil except over land actually cultivated or fenced in for that purpose."

5. The first white Australians tried for the murder of Aborigines (at Myall

Creek in 1838) were pursued and arrested by the police magistrate of Maitland, Captain Edward Denny Day (the author's great grandfather). They were subsequently executed notwithstanding vehement opposition voiced by the *Sydney Herald* and sections of an ambivalent colonial community.

6. Roberts, Stephen, 1924, *History of Australian Land Settlement*, Macmillan, Melbourne; revised and reprinted 1968 (460 pp.). At p. 105 there is an interesting reference to proposals in 1831 by Under-Secretary Goderich (Viscount Ripon) to enforce quit-rents and to substitute for improvement clauses a small tax on all uncultivated land—"the first proposal in Australia for taxation of unimproved values."

7. Justice Rae Else-Mitchell, 1974, *Legacies of the Nineteenth Century Land Reformers from Melville to George*, UQ Press, Brisbane.

8. State valuation authorities value land for the purposes of municipal rates and state land tax and as a basis for compensation when land is acquired or resumed for public purposes. (State land taxes, however, are not a true land value tax but are wealth taxes levied above variable and arbitrarily determined thresholds.)

9. Some years ago in Victoria, where local government councils had the option of using improved or unimproved land values as a rating base, Georgist researchers sought to show that Melbourne suburban councils that rated on unimproved land values experienced greater economic activity. The data lacked conviction, however, partly because of the relatively insignificant monetary impact of municipal rates, and partly because higher aggregate building approvals in some outer suburban councils simply reflected the natural growth of newly developing areas.

"Ground rents are a species of revenue which
the owner enjoys without any care of attention
of his own and can best bear to have a
peculiar tax imposed upon them."
—Adam Smith

"The whole of the people have the right to the
ownership of land and the right to share in the
value of land itself, though not to share in the
fruits of the land which properly belong to the
individuals by whose labour they are produced."
—Alfred Deakin

References

Andelson, R. V., ed. 1979. *Critics of Henry George.* Associated University Presses, New Jersey and London.

Australian Institute of Urban Studies. 1972. *The Price of Land.* Canberra.

Australian Local Government Association. 1993. *Local Government Urban Strategy.* Canberra.

Brisbane City Council. 1989. *Report of the Committee of Inquiry into Valuation and Rating.*

Churchill, W. S. 1970. *The People's Rights.* Jonathan Cape, London. (first published 1909).

Commissioner of Taxation. 1994. *Annual Report 1993–1994.* AGPS, Canberra.

Commonwealth of Australia. 1936. *Income Tax Assessment Act* (as amended). Australian Government Publishing Service, Canberra.

——. 1974. *Commission of Inquiry into Land Tenures.* AGPS, Canberra.

——. 1993. *Native Title Act* (as amended). AGPS, Canberra.

Commonwealth Treasury. 1994. *Tax Law Improvement Project.* AGPS, Canberra.

Day, P. D. 1982. *Planning and Development: The Philosophy and Practice of Development Contributions.* Australian Institute of Urban Studies, Canberra.

——. 1992. *Land Value Capture.* Local Government Association of Queensland, Brisbane.

Economic Planning Advisory Council. 1993. *Income Tax and Asset Choice in Australia.* Research Paper No. 34, AGPS, Canberra.

Else-Mitchell, R. 1974. *Legacies of the Nineteenth Century Land Reformers from Melville to George.* University of Queensland Press, Brisbane.

George, Henry. 1879. *Progress and Poverty.* Centenary edition, Hogarth Press, London. 1979.

Griffith, Samuel. 1890. Bill for an Act *The Elementary Property Law of Queensland. Queensland Parliamentary Debates,* Legislative Assembly, 1890, Vols. 61 and 62. See also: Murphy, D. and Joyce, R. B. 1978. *Queensland Political Portraits 1859–1952.* University of Queensland Press, Brisbane.

Harrison, F. 1983. *The Power in the Land.* Universe Books, New York.

Heilbroner, R. 1980. *The Worldly Philosophers.* Simon and Schuster, New York.

Industry Commission. 1993. *Taxation and Financial Policy Impacts on Urban Settlement,* Vol. 1. AGPS, Canberra.

Jackson and McConnell. 1985. *Economics.* McGraw-Hill, Sydney.

Kavanagh, B. 1993. *The Recovery Myth.* Land Values Research Group, Box 2688X, GPO, Melbourne.

Kemeny, J. 1983. *The Great Australian Nightmare.* Georgian House, Melbourne.

Mabo and Others v. Queensland (No.2). 1992. 176 Commonwealth Law Reports.

Marx, K. 1848. *Das Kapital* (Book 3).

New South Wales. 1967. *Report of the Royal Commission of Inquiry into Rating, Valuation and Local Government Finance.* NSW Government Printer.

——. 1975. *Planning and Environment Commission Report.* NSW Government Printer.

Prest, A. R. 1981. *The Taxation of Urban Land.* Manchester University Press.

Roberts, Stephen. 1924. *History of Australian Land Settlement.* Macmillan, Melbourne. Revised and reprinted 1968.

Rogers, J. Thorold. 1919. *Six Centuries of Work and Wages—The History of English Labour.* Fisher Unwin, London.

Samuelson et al. 1992. *Economics.* McGraw-Hill, Sydney.

Sandercock, L. 1975. *Cities for Sale.* Melbourne University Press.

——. 1979. *The Land Racket.* Australian Association of Socialist Studies, Melbourne.

Schumpeter, J. 1954. *A History of Economic Analysis.* Oxford University Press.

Sen, Amartya. 1994. "Population: Delusion and Reality," *New York Review,* 22.9.94.

Smith, Adam. 1776. *An Inquiry into the Nature and Causes of the Wealth of Nations.* Dent & Sons, Everyman's Library, 1971.

Standard Hours Case. 1947. Arbitration Commission Proceedings, 21.5.47.

Stretton, H. 1989. *Ideas for Australian Cities.* Transit Australia Publishing, Sydney.

United Kingdom. 1947. *Town and Country Planning Act.* H. M. Stationery Office.

United Nations. 1976. *Recommendations of the United Nations Conference for National Action on Human Settlements* (Habitat). "The Vancouver Plan."

Wik Peoples v. Queensland; Thayorre People v. Queensland. 1996. 141 Australian Law Reports.

Autobiographical Sketch of Philip Denny Day (1924–)

Land owes nothing to a precise moment of revelation or intuitive conviction. Instead, experience acquired variously, and largely fortuitously, in public administration, urban and regional planning and development, and multidisciplinary academic inquiry gradually led me over time to a realization that puzzling features of contemporary attitudes to land and property and public revenue raising were seemingly embedded in a curiously pervasive mindset.

Born in Brisbane, Australia, I graduated in law from the University of Queensland in 1953 after seven years in the Australian Army, three of them as an army-trained Japanese linguist in the British Commonwealth Occupation Force in Japan, latterly with a commission in the Intelligence Corps. After graduation, I was admitted to the Queensland Bar, but chose instead to join the Commonwealth Public Service in Canberra (where, as an extracurricular activity, I served two terms as an elected member of the Australian Capital Territory Advisory Council, the modest vehicle of community representation in the days before the federal capital territory became self-governing).

For one entering the Commonwealth Service later than the more immediate postwar entrants, the promotional prospects seemed limited. I moved to New South Wales in 1959, acquiring some experience in the real estate industry before studying town and country planning at Sydney University under the inspirational Denis Winston and joining the NSW Department of Local Government. Working in state government closer to real people rather than at a distance in the more remote national government in Canberra was refreshing, and the introduction to the many dimensions of town and country planning was intensely interesting and intellectually stimulating. As a profession, town planning was still emerging; town planners were few on the ground in state and local government, and early planning schemes were unsophisticated documents. As a relatively junior officer, I found myself hearing town planning appeals throughout NSW on behalf of the local government minister pursuant to an appeals system modeled on that in the United Kingdom. Looking back, transcribing (unassisted) the parties' oral submissions and analyzing the always different planning circumstances was demanding, but drafting reports afterwards while contemplating the passing scenery courtesy of the NSW railways was often pleasantly satisfying.

After some unrelated but similarly interesting experience in the Department of Labour and Industry's industrial information bureau, I joined the Department of Decentralisation and Development, becoming Deputy Director and later Director at a time when decentralization and regional development were becoming lively issues. This was coincident with the advent in 1972 of the activist Whitlam Labor government in Canberra, which was committed to the promotion of selected growth centers, land commissions, and wide-ranging socioeconomic reform. I was the editor and main author of the NSW department's landmark *Report on Selective Decentralisation, The Regional Organisation Report,* and the NSW supplement to the Commonwealth/State Officials Committee *Report on Decentralisation.*

When the promising initiatives of the turbulent early 1970s were stalled by intergovernmental conflict, I returned to Queensland in 1974, briefly as Director of Town Planning with the Brisbane City Council before joining the University of Queensland Department of Regional and Town Planning and subsequently succeeding the inimitable Lewis Keeble as head. It was a time for vigorously propagating the objectives of town planning in the inhospitable political climate that then prevailed in Queensland and, later in the 1980s, that was reflected within the University of Queensland hierarchy.

I enjoyed two years' secondment as Director of the Australian Institute of Urban Studies in Canberra before retiring from UQ in 1988 and continuing community activism in a private capacity, along with some governmental commissions and active membership of the Royal Australian Planning Institute and editorship for 16 years of its journal *Queensland Planner.*

The chronological biographical minutiae, however, are not important. Disparate influences led to an awareness of the special significance of land and natural resources and eventually, in midlife, to seeing the kaleidoscopic Georgist cat.[1] At the University of Queensland, I lectured in planning law and regional planning and some introductory land economics. By the 1980s, in the course of observing the formative years of town planning in the Australian states, I had become aware that the planning system was fatally flawed unless it captured the windfall land value profits conferred upon landowners by the granting of permission; but that the evolving practice of extracting development contributions had no very clear rationale. A particularly significant involvement was membership in the Committee of Inquiry into Valuation and Rating appointed by the lord mayor of Brisbane (pop. 800,000; area 1,200 square kilometers). The committee's exhaustive two-volume report in 1989 confirmed that, for Brisbane, a rate levied on the unimproved capital value of land was the most equitable and efficient source of general revenue (apart from user charges and license fees). Significantly, the committee endorsed this approach to revenue raising "irrespective of the level of government."

My role in this inquiry led to an invitation to become a trustee of the Henry George Foundation of Australia and join in the propagation of the Georgist cause (and read, for the first time, *Progress and Poverty*). I was the Australian member of an international Georgist group that visited Russia in 1993, and I was the principal author of a comprehensive submission to a tax reform "summit" in Canberra in 1996. However I became disillusioned with the HGFA's reiterative endorsement of the single tax; its seeming entrapment since 1879 in a complacent time warp; and above all, its failure to systematically identify and realistically address the practical, political, and ingrained cultural obstacles that frustrate greater recourse to land value taxation in contemporary federal Australia.

Contemporaneously with numerous media and journal articles, *Planning and Development: The Philosophy and Practice of Development Contributions* was published in 1982, *Land Value Capture* in 1992, and *Land: The Elusive Quest for Social Justice, Taxation Reform and a Sustainable Planetary Environment* in 1995. The augmented edition of *Land* draws upon a transdisciplinary doctoral thesis that reviewed the evolution of Anglo-Australian land law and fiscal practice following the decline of feudalism and the enshrinement of individual profit seeking in a capitalist economy.

Philip Denny Day, November 20, 2004

Note

1. Students of Georgist economic thought confess to a "moment" when the basic intuitions of Henry George become their own intuitions. Forever after, they see the world of politics and economics differently than they had seen it before. Georgists have a way of memorializing this moment in time as "seeing the cat." The reference is to a puzzle in which the image of a ordinary feline is camouflaged in some way and then, after staring at the puzzle for some time, the cat suddenly appears in a Gestalt experience.—Ed.

Index

A

ability-to-pay principle, 45
Abercrombie, Sir Patrick, 39
Aboriginal and tribal societies, 6
Aboriginal land rights movement,
    101, 102
adversarial system, 22
America, *see* United States
Andelson, Robert, 85–88, 92, 107
annual rental value, 43, 44, 46, 47,
    50, 51, 53, 57, 61–63, 66, 69,
    71, 92, 96
    see also land, value rental
appeals
    against land use decisions, 17, 22,
        32, 62, 113
    against rental assessments, 62
Aquino, C., 77
Arbitration Court, 20
Association for Land Value Taxation,
    88
Australia, 2–6, 14–21, 25–27, 30, 31,
    35, 37, 39, 40, 42, 43, 45, 47,
    48, 50, 51, 66, 69, 70, 73, 88,
    95, 96, 99–105, 111, 113
    Australian Army, 111
    Australian Capital Territory (ACT),
        14, 17, 22, 40, 71, 103, 111
    Australian Constitution, 62, 106
    Australian High Court, 20, 101,
        104
    Australian Institute of Urban
        Studies, 22, 109, 112
    Australian Local Government
        Association, 23, 109
    Australian tax system, 25, 35
    Australian Taxation Office, 35, 48,
        68
    Brisbane, 12, 45–47, 49, 71, 109,
        111–113
    Brisbane City Council, 12, 45,
        109, 112
    Canberra, 62, 63, 103, 111–113
    Canberra Times, 32
    Darling, Governor, 103
    Elementary Property Law of
        Queensland, 104
    Gipps, Governor, 103
    Henry George Foundation of
        Australia, 113
    *Mabo and Others v. Queensland
        (No. 2)*, 59, 101, 110
    Macquarie, Governor, 102
    Melbourne, 26
    Nelly Bay, 32
    New South Wales (NSW), 14, 17,
        18, 40, 71, 102–104, 110, 111,
        112
        NSW Department of Local
            Government, 111
        NSW Planning and
            Environment Commission, 15
        NSW Royal Commission of
            Inquiry into Rating, Valuation
            and Local
            Government Finance, 15
    Royal Australian Planning
        Institute, 112
    Queensland, 17, 23, 32, 66, 71,
        101–104, 111, 112
    Queensland Planner, 112
    South Australia, 66
    Sydney, 14
    Sydney Cove, 102
    Thayorre People v. Queensland,
        101
    Victoria, 17, 22, 71, 72, 103, 107
    Western Australia, 102
    Wik Peoples v. Queensland, 101

B

benefit principle, 45, 46, 72
Birmingham, 11
bureaucratic inertia, 90
Better Cities Program, 21
betterment, 3–5, 14, 15, 17, 20, 21,
    22, 25, 40–42, 84, 100,
    105
Brisbane, 12, 45–47, 49, 71, 109,
    111–113

Brisbane City Council, 12, 45, 109, 112
British Commonwealth Occupation Force, 111

C
Cameron, Clyde, 28
Canberra, 62, 63, 103, 111–113
Canberra Times, 32
capital gains tax, 25, 37
capitalism, 7, 55, 75, 79, 87, 92
    apprehension re Western-style capitalism, 55
Catholic Church, 87
Cathrein, Victor, 87
Christianity, 89
Churchill, Winston, 83, 84, 109
Cobden, Richard, 83
Commission of Inquiry into Land Tenures, 15, 42
Committee of Inquiry into Valuation and Rating, 45–47, 113
Commonwealth Treasury, 27, 38, 50, 109
"community charge," 71, 80
compensation, 5, 8, 15, 42, 83, 84, 91, 100, 103, 107
compliance costs, 35–37, 45, 46, 48, 81
"confiscation," 65, 79, 80, 88
consumption tax on land, 50
Cook, Captain James, 101, 106
Crown, 6, 42, 52, 101, 103, 106

D
Darling, Governor, 103
Das Kapital, 76
Day, Captain Edward Denny, 107
Day, Philip Denny (autobiographical sketch), 111–113
Deakin, Alfred, 96, 107
deferment of charges against land, 62, 67
development contributions, 15–21, 40, 113
development industry, 4, 16, 18, 19, 40, 44, 52, 65, 90

distinction between land, site and unimproved capital values, 43, 46, 47, 69, 71, 113
diversion of investment, 25–28, 89
Domesday Book, 104
domino effect, 13
Dusseldorp, Gerardus, 52

E
Eastern Europe, 7
Economic Planning Advisory Council (EPAC), 5, 25, 109
Elementary Property Law of Queensland, 104
elimination of land price, 44
elimination of taxes, 48, 51, 57, 69
England, *see* United Kingdom
Else-Mitchell, Judge Rae, 52, 103, 107, 109
employment
    see also unemployment
    mirage of, 29–32
environmental conservation, 1, 57
environmental implications and impacts, 12, 19

F
Fairhall, Sir Allen, 28
farmers, 56, 66
feudal system, 6, 77, 113
fiscal masochism, 35–37
foreign ownership of land, 63
former Soviet Union, 7, 55
Foster, Judge, 20
France, 77
    French Physiocrats, 77
    French Revolution, 77
free enterprise, principles of, 4
fringe benefits tax, 35, 36

G
Gear, George, 38
George, Henry, 73–84, 85–89, 93, 97, 103, 109, 113, 114
Gipps, Governor, 103
Glasgow, 11
Gostroi, 56
governmental inertia, 105
Greater London Plan, 39

Griffith, Sir Samuel, 96, 103, 104, 109
GST, 99

H
Harrison, Fred, 28, 93, 109
Heilbroner, Robert, 93, 109
Henry George Foundation of Australia, 113
home ownership, 25, 26
housing affordability, 13, 19
Huxley, T. H., 86

I
impact fees, 19, 20
implementation and staging of land value rental, 70, 97
import restrictions, 33
improved capital value, 43, 46, 47, 69, 71
incentive to "develop," 19, 52, 65, 100
income tax, 6, 25, 35–37, 48, 49, 51, 66–68, 70, 93, 99
Income Tax Assessment Act, 6, 35
Industrial Revolution, 76
Industry Commission, 5, 8, 22, 109
inequality, 1, 7, 21, 29, 30, 68, 69, 74, 77, 82, 89, 92, 96, 97, 106
"information society," the, 68
injurious affection, 8, 43
investment, diversion of, 25–27

J
Jackson & McConnell, 94, 109
Japan, 33, 111
Johannesburg, 40

K
Kavanagh, Bryan, 28, 109
Keeble, Lewis, 112
Kondratieff, Nikolai, 28
Kyoto Protocol, 99, 100

L
land
  nationalisation, 41, 42, 49, 65, 83, 86

tax, 2, 6, 25, 37, 50, 53, 66, 67, 70, 72, 83, 93, 107
use, 3, 4, 8, 10, 12, 13, 15, 18, 37, 39–44, 46, 51–53, 57, 62, 90, 92, 105
value rental, 50, 51, 57, 58, 65, 66, 68–71, 77, 87–89, 92, 94, 96, 97
Land Tenures Report, 42
Land Values Research Group, 26–28, 53
landed wealth cumulative, 7, 86
Leo XIII, Pope, 87
lifestyle, 30–33, 78, 96
local government rating, 2, 6, 21, 47, 53, 72, 100, 104
London, 11
long wave theory, 28

M
Mabo, Eddie, 101
Mabo and Others v. Queensland (No. 2), 59, 101, 110
Macquarie, Governor, 102
Malthus, Thomas, 73, 78, 83, 86
Malthusian dilemma, 20th-century variation on, 30
Maori chiefs, 103
Marx, Karl, 58, 75, 76, 110
Marxism, 57, 58, 75, 76, 87–89
Mathews, Russell, 52
Melbourne, 26
Middle Ages, 6, 105
monopolisation, 86
morality, 14, 55–59, 82, 91, 92
Moscow, 55
most efficient and equitable revenue base, 46
Murray Island, 101

N
National Capital Planning Authority, 5
national taxation authorities, 81
National Tax Summit, 88
nationalisation of land, 41, 42, 49, 65, 83, 86
Native Title Act, 101
negative gearing, 25, 27
Nelly Bay, 32

neo-liberal economic ideology, 105
Neo-Malthusianism, 78
New South Wales (NSW), 14, 17, 18, 40, 71, 102–104, 110, 111, 112
 NSW Department of Local Government, 111
 NSW Planning and Environment Commission, 15
 NSW Royal Commission of Inquiry into Rating, Valuation and Local Government Finance, 15
New York, 88
New Zealand, 40, 73, 93, 103

O
O'Malley, King, 96

P
Palgrave's Dictionary of Political Economy, 79
PAYE taxpayers disadvantaged, 36, 38
payroll tax, 37, 48, 70, 72
penalising of work and enterprise, 1, 7, 37, 39, 45, 49, 50, 71, 89, 90
Physiocrats, the, 77
Planning and Environment Court, 17
"planning gain," 13, 16, 18
planning, principles of, 10, 12
population growth, 2, 7, 13, 21, 31, 41, 78, 79, 87, 94
Prest, A. R., 28, 110
principles of equity and efficiency, 23
privatisation, 31, 55, 56, 105
profiteering
 see also windfall profits
 institutional, 9–21
Progress and Poverty, 73, 74, 77, 79, 85, 86, 88, 113
public revenue
 see also tax and taxation
 resourcing, 39–52
public works, impact on values, 1, 2, 5, 11, 14, 20, 47

Q
Queensland, 17, 23, 32, 66, 71, 101–104, 111, 112
Queensland Planner, 112
Quiggin, John, 32, 33
quit-rent, 6, 71, 103, 107

R
Racial Discrimination Act, 101
reason, subversion of, 1–8
Rerum Novarum, 87
Reserve Bank, 27
revenue potential of land value rental, 45, 47
Ricardo, David, 78
Roberts, Sir Stephen, 102, 107
Rogers, J. E. Thorold, 77, 82, 83, 110
Roman Catholic Church, 87
Roman law, 77
Royal Commission of Inquiry into Rating, Valuation & Local Government Finance (NSW), 15
royalties, 37, 94
Russia, 55–58, 113
 Gostroi, 56
 Moscow, 55
 Union of Russian Cities, 56

S
sales tax, 6, 35, 46, 48
Samuelson, P. et al., 93, 110
Sandercock, Leonie, 93, 110
Schumpeter, Joseph, 86, 87, 110
Scotland, *see* United Kingdom
Sen, Amartya, 83, 110
"single tax," 49, 79, 87, 93, 97, 113
Smith, Adam, 76, 77, 86, 107, 110
societal inertia, 70, 105
South Australia, 66
Soviet Union (former), 7, 55
Stalinists, 57
stamp duty, 53, 72
Standard Hours case, 23, 110
standard of living, 31
Stretton, Hugh, 28, 110
subsidies, 4, 11, 19, 28, 44, 94
sumptuary taxes, 49
sustainable development, 13, 18, 82

Sydney, 14
Sydney Cove, 102

T
Tasmania, 22
tax and taxation
    Australian system of, 25, 35, 48,
        69, 99
    Australian Taxation Office, 35, 48,
        68
    avoidance and evasion, 37, 39, 81
    betterment, 25
    capital gains, 25, 37, 38, 69
    company/corporation, 50
    complexity of law of, 36, 38, 62,
        109
    consumption, 50
    fringe benefits, 35, 36
    goods and services, 50, 99
    government needs met by, 6
    GST, 99
    improved property value, 46
    income, 7, 36, 37, 46, 48, 49, 50,
        51, 66–70, 93, 99
    Income Tax Assessment Act, 6, 35
    land, 6, 25, 46, 66, 67, 72, 76, 83,
        87, 88, 93
    land value, 46, 104, 107, 113
    National Tax Summit, 88
    national taxing authorities, 81
    payroll, 37, 48, 70, 72
    penalization of productivity by, 2,
        5, 7, 18, 39, 56, 89
    philosophy and principles of, 45,
        46, 77, 93, 96
    poll, 46, 63
    private consumption of
        community resource, 7, 37,
        50
    property, 55, 63
    sales, 6, 35, 46, 48
    "single," 49, 79, 87, 93, 97, 113
    state land, 2, 6, 37, 50, 53, 67, 70,
        107
    sumptuary, 49
    Tax Law Improvement Project, 36
    unimproved value of land, 22, 46,
        107
    wealth, 46, 67, 69, 72, 107
    wholesale, 37, 99

Tax Law Improvement Project, 36
Thayorre People v. Queensland, 101
Tolstoy, Count Leo, 56, 79
Town and Country Planning Act
    (UK), 22, 42
town planning, 2–4, 9–15, 19, 22,
    39–41, 46, 52, 56, 57, 61, 81,
    90, 91, 100, 105, 111–113
Transvaal, 40

U
unearned wealth, 74, 75, 95, 97
unearned windfall profit, 43
unemployment
    alleviating, 29, 31
    ameliorating, 29
    causes of, 30, 44, 106
    import restrictions and, 33
    inequality and unfairness, as form
        of, 29
    land rental increases, effect of on
        those experiencing, 51
    levels of, 32
    nature and implications of, 31
    payroll tax and, 37
    reduction of, 30, 32
    structural, 1, 78
unimproved land value, 15, 22, 40,
    43, 46, 47, 50, 63, 66, 67, 69,
    71, 72, 89, 104, 107, 113
Union of Russian Cities, 56
unique character of land, 14, 75
United Kingdom, 11, 12, 14–16, 18,
    21, 27, 28, 42, 63, 77, 83,
    103–105, 110, 111
    Birmingham, 11
    British Commonwealth
        Occupation Force, 111
    Glasgow, 11
    Greater London Plan, 39
    London, 11
    Town and Country Planning Act,
        22, 42
United Nations Habitat Conference
    on Human Settlements (the
    Vancouver Plan), 3, 15, 110
United States, 5, 15, 19, 73, 79, 103,
    104
    New York, 88
"unjust enrichment," 39

urban blight, 71
urban sprawl, 3, 14, 20, 89, 104
user charges, 49, 53, 72
Uthwatt Commission, 84

V
valuations, up-to-date, importance
    of, 15, 62
valuers, 43, 56, 68, 72, 104
Vancouver Plan, 3, 15, 110
Victoria, 17, 22, 71, 72, 103, 107

W
Wentworth, W. C., 103
Western Australia, 102

Western society, 4, 6, 7, 10, 11, 15,
    30, 55–58, 62, 65, 77, 90, 91,
    96, 105
Whitehall, 102
Whitlam labor government, 112
Wik Peoples v. Queensland, 101
windfall profits, 1–6, 17, 18, 20, 23,
    30, 32, 38, 39, 40, 43, 68, 81,
    82, 113
Winston, Denis, 111
wipeouts, 5, 8
woodchip export controversy, 32
World Bank, 57
World War II, 37
"worsenment," 3, 40–42